MOUNT[...]
BIKE G[...]
West Yorkshire

by
NICK DUTTON-TAYLOR

ERNEST

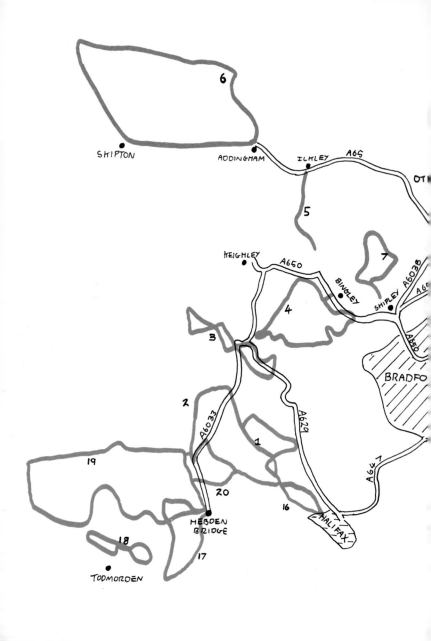

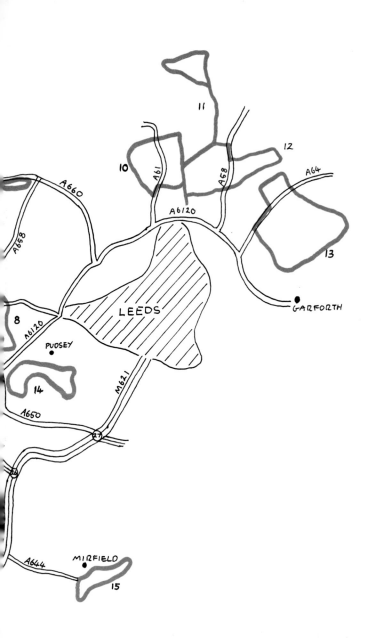

CONTENTS

ACKNOWLEDGEMENTS

As is customary in such publications, I feel that I should thank people who have given me assistance. If your name does not appear below and you feel that you have been a great source of help and advice and that the book would not have made it to the publishers without your help, then I apologise and leave a blank space at the bottom of the page for you to fill in your name. I would, however, like to point out that standing next to me in a queue at Morrisons is not actually that useful. So here goes: thanks to....

My wife Amanda, for generally putting up with my wild schemes and making me a kept man; Sam for just being so damn cute; John Howard for being the sort of person that mends Citroens and always has a happy word or two for a weary traveller; Jez Spencer for looking like the lead singer from Right Said Fred and keeping me amused with his mud depth-testing antics and complete lack of balance; Lifecycle International for providing the life saving and terrifically accurate pink Avocet 40; Matthew Peacock at Ellis Briggs for advice and bits; everyone at Aire Valley Cycles for technical advice and just being generally useful; Cyclesport Batley for ditto; the nice people at Orange for being helpful even though they are busy (it's nice to see manufacturers taking an interest in the sport apart from the money side); Giles for coming with me on routes; Jim (I do not know your surname) for the same and especially the various people at the Countryside Services: Rick Hill, Chris Dean, Neville Herron, Richard Welbourn, Richard Bows, for their invaluable help.

The publishers wish to acknowledge help with photographs from Cathy Carter of Pace (Research) Cycles Ltd., and to Susan Hodgkiss for editorial and production supervision.

INTRODUCTION

West Yorkshire is extremely well-placed for Mountain Biking: having easy access to the Yorkshire Dales, The Peak District and even the Lake District and the North Yorks Moors – the potential for good routes is immense.

As more and more mountain bikers search further and further afield for the ultimate mountain bike route, it seems that many have overlooked the potential that lies on their own doorstep.

This book is an attempt to raise cyclists' awareness of the possibilities in their own environment of a rich source of entertainment and also an opportunity to rediscover their surroundings.

This book was written with several aims in mind. Firstly, for those who have their own transport, it is an opportunity to go for a decent ride without the 100 mile round trip that accompanies it. For those who do not have access to transport, a guide to local routes will open up new avenues, especially as most of the rides in the guidebook can be reached using public transport.

Secondly, the variety and range of challenges offered by these routes are enormous and quite surprising. Within the guidebook there are routes offering gentle introductions that will suit novice riders as well as more technically and physically demanding routes for the more experienced.

Thirdly, the book also aims to provide a readily accessible reference of good, legal, local routes thus encouraging people to ride more responsibly and minimising the effect that irresponsible riders have on the reputation of the sport.

Last but definitely not least, it aims to help people get more enjoyment out of the sport; after all most of us are out there to have fun.

ENVIRONMENT

West Yorkshire is a county of great diversity: regarded by many people, usually those who have never visited, as an industrial sprawl, all cloth caps and wippets, the reality is rather different. Certainly, West Yorkshire has an industrial history. There are constant reminders of this as one travels around, and this is very much what has shaped the area. However, to me the beauty of the area lies in its landscape. It does not matter where you are, you can always see the green of the hills, even from the cities, helping to lessen that claustrophobic feel that many urban areas have. Once out of the towns, you are soon able to forget them as you travel for miles through beautiful countryside. Enough of waxing lyrical. The routes in this book reflect the variety and beauty of the area and may help people to get to know it a little better – it is worth the effort.

The county has a wide range of terrain open to mountain bikers of all ability and also has the advantage of an excellent communications network.

The western side of the county around Halifax and Bradford, is essentially Pennine Yorkshire. This area, generally rugged and hilly with hill farming the norm and with its textile history, is a particularly fertile area for mountain biking with many good and interesting routes providing both physically and technically demanding riding. As you move east, things calm down a bit so that by the time you get out to the east of Leeds, the land is much more gentle and rolling with more dairy and arable farming near the vale of York; still however providing challenging and interesting routes. Points in between are really a mixture of both and the only real blight is the Kirklees and Wakefield areas in the south-east which offer very little in the way of routes due to their distinct lack of bridleways.

Thus, the area has a lot to offer anybody with a bike regardless of ability or ambition and if the area in which you live is not really demanding enough, do not be disheartened – there will be somewhere close at hand.

With all these routes, as on any mountain biking route, it is of the utmost importance that you respect the environment in which you ride. It all comes down to common sense: the Off Road Code below lays out the basics but they really are the basics. Remember that all the land you use is owned by somebody and that many of the tracks are maintained by a lot of hard work. Much of the land provides a living for its owners. In addition to the Off Road Code, please use your head and try to minimise the impact which you have on the environment. Many of the routes cover fragile, peaty terrain, fine in the summer when it is hard-packed and dry, but in the winter after heavy rain, many of the routes, or sections of them can become quagmires. If the weather has been bad, please do not use the route – there are plenty to choose from. Most of the routes that are particularly susceptible to bogginess are highlighted in their accompanying text.

THE OFF ROAD CODE
Issued by The British Mountain Bike Federation.
Only ride where you know you have legal right.
Always give way to horses and walkers.
Avoid animals and crops. In some circumstances this may not be possible, at which times contact should be kept to a minimum.
Take all litter with you.
Leave all gates as found.
Keep noise down.
Do not get annoyed with anyone; it never solves any problems.
Always try to be self sufficient, for you and your bike.
Never create a fire hazard.

EQUIPMENT
Although most of the routes are near largely populated areas, this does not mean that you are less isolated in case of accident or emergency. Many of the routes pass within sight of houses

but these are not frequently used, especially midweek. Thus, treat any ride as you would a day out in the dales – a little preparation and equipment could solve a lot of problems. Below is a list of equipment which may be useful. Not all items are vital.

Bike:
A fairly important piece of kit but one often sadly neglected. Make sure that checks are regularly made, specifically for things like brake efficiency and wear, tyre wear. Check all cables, particularly well hidden ones and make sure all nuts etc are tight. Check these details BEFORE you go out.

Tool kit:
A good tool kit can save a lot of hassle and aggravation. A few basic items which you should carry for the more frequent mishaps are: tyre levers, puncture repair kit, pump, universal spanner, Allen keys, chain splitter, screwdriver and if possible some grease/lube. For longer runs or if you have room, other useful items are: spare tubes, spare cable, spoke adjuster etc. Obviously you will not be prepared for every eventuality unless you decide to take with you a complete tool kit, welding torch, work stand and a team of fully trained mechanics, but you will be able to cope with most and it is usually the little things that cause the biggest hassle.

Clothing:
The most important item of clothing is of course a HELMET. The basic rule is, DO NOT RIDE WITHOUT ONE. As far as the rest of it goes, you do not need to be a Lycra Fetishist, although it is rather nice, but a decent pair of padded shorts can be very useful. Other than this, a pair of gloves, some decent footwear, and a good waterproof are all you really need. The main rule is to be comfortable and to be able to control your heat well.

Maps: See next section.

Water:
Dehydration can be really dangerous. Fit a water bottle and drink plenty.

Food:
Particularly on the longer and more isolated routes, food needs to be taken both for energy and for survival in case of accident.

MAPS:

Each route covered in this book is accompanied by its own sketch-map. These maps are not intended to be fully comprehensive but a simplification of reality and a useful reference point to accompany the text.

These sketch-maps are not sufficient used alone and you should refer to the relevant Ordnance Survey maps for the area for more detailed information.

The most useful maps are the Pathfinder (Green Cover) series. These were used in the writing of this book and their 1:25000 scale is ideal for mountain bikers. For routes in the east, around Hebden Bridge, a larger, although same scale, map from the Outdoor Leisure series is available (No. 21). Again, these maps are not sufficient when on a route. **I therefore strongly recommend** that, before setting out, you read through the route description. Using this information and the hand-drawn sketch-map, you will be able to plot your route on the O.S. map. (I used a yellow highlighter pen to mark out all the routes.) This little exercise will make route-finding and navigation a lot easier and safer.

Due to their expense, I would think it unlikely that anyone would need to buy a full set of Pathfinder maps, although it may be useful to obtain ones for your local area.

A word of warning. Just because routes are marked on a map as a Bridleway this is no evidence of right of way. Bridleways change and many of the maps for the area are 10 years old or more. If in doubt, please check up before you ride. The Countryside services for each area are a good source of information for this purpose.

Actual maps (with route no. in brackets) are:–

PATHFINDER:
661 Skipton and Hellifield (6)
662 Bolton Abbey and Blubberhouses (6)
671 Keighley and Ilkley (3, 5, 7, 9)
672 Harewood (9, 10, 11, 12)
682 Bradford (W.Yorks) (3, 4, 7, 8)
683 Leeds (8, 13, 14)
684 Garforth and Sherburn in Elmet (13)
703 Wakefield (South) and Area (15)

OUTDOOR LEISURE:
 21 South Pennines (1, 2, 16, 17, 18, 19, 20)

CONSERVATION:

A very topical subject at the moment, I feel that it is important to mention conservation and stress again the need for responsible riding in order to help lessen the effect on the environment in which you ride.

As well as just riding carefully, there are other things which you could do in order to help look after your environment.

In West Yorkshire, we are very lucky in that we have a network of extremely efficient and active Countryside Officers who deal with rights of way and the general upkeep of bridleways and footpaths. These people are in general very sympathetic to the needs of the mountain biker and are willing to do what they can in order to help. However, as is usually the case, their resources and manpower do not always let them do what they would like to. To this end, most of the areas have volunteer schemes for people who would like to put something back into the environ-

11

ment. It would be nice if mountain bikers were seen to be helping out as well. Below is a list of telephone numbers for the Countryside services for each area. Please give them a hand.

BRADFORD
    HAWORTH (0535) 647092

LEEDS
    (0532) 326871

TONG-CALVERLEY COUNTRYSIDE PROJECT
    (0532) 753516

OTLEY CHEVIN
    (0943) 465023

CALDERDALE
    (0422) 886149

EXPLANATION OF THE ROUTES

The routes in this book are intended in their variety to reflect the diversity of both the area and the cyclist who will use the book.

To be included in the book, routes have to meet several criteria:
– they have to start in W Yorks or be very near the border.
– the majority of the route has to be rideable.
– with the exception of the urban routes, at least half the route must be off road (this does not include access to the route via public transport).
– routes where possible should be accessible to people without access to their own transport.

The routes have all been ridden by me at least twice and in many cases more than that. I have often been accompanied on the second run in order to check the details. Distances have been measured using my extremely groovy and very pink Avocet 40 computer (thankyou Lifecycle) and are pretty accurate, although some figures have been rounded up or down to simplify. I am an average mountain biker; although I have been doing it for nearly 4 years, I have only become serious quite recently. Thus, if I say a route is physically demanding that means that I found it so. Therefore, superfit athletes may find them easy and may do them a lot quicker; and pie-munchers may find them harder and may take longer – it is only a guide!

The routes are all of different lengths, severity and technicality. Attempts have been made to find routes that are suitable for all riders. Thus, all routes have been given a twofold grading system based on Physical Difficulty (PD) and Technical Difficulty (TD) and appear in that order in the route headings.

All routes have been checked with the relevant authorities (in most cases the local Countryside Commission) to check for legality and possible points of friction. Thus, at the time of going to press, all routes are legally rideable all the way to the best of my knowledge. However, the existence of a route in this book is not evidence of a legal right of way. As situations and needs change, bridleways can be downgraded to footpath status and vice versa. During the making of this book, several new routes have been opened up which did not exist when I started, and unfortunately several that were planned, no longer exist. I am also aware of plans which may affect one or two of the routes (for the better) by adding more to them. As and when routes change, they will be clearly signposted by the local authorities.

HOW TO USE THE GUIDE

For each route, there is an introduction giving a brief description of the route and the type of ride; technical information, showing distance, height gained etc; directions, detailed information on navigating the route and a sketch-map.

Thus, each route has enough information for the reader firstly to decide which one to do and then how to follow it.

The introduction is only intended as a very brief overview of the route, mentioning the general terrain, particular features and anything else that came in to my mind whilst writing.

The technical information is a brief analysis of the most important details in planning which route to use. All routes have been given a twofold grading based on Physical Difficulty (PD) and Technical Difficulty (TD), each of which is rated from 1–5 with one being the easiest. PD refers to the amount of physical ability a rider needs to complete a route. Thus, a low PD would possibly be a short route with few uphill climbs, and a high PD may mean that it is either very long or has a lot of climbing. TD refers to the technical ability required by the cyclist. Thus, a high TD would mean rough, difficult to ride tracks where a high degree of skill is needed, and a low TD would be suitable for novices. The combination of these 2 measures should help to provide the best route for you.

Distances are measured in miles and the split between on and off road is approximate.

Height gain is in feet (I do not understand metric) and is the distance between the lowest point of the route and the highest. It is not cumulative.

Time is the amount of time it should take a reasonably fit person to complete the run (based on the amount of time it took me). On the longer runs, this included a brief stop for lunch. They are only meant to be guides.

Further information is provided to help get an idea of the physical feel of the run and advises which map to take along.

The directions are intended to be detailed enough for you to feel confident without having to count every blade of grass and every sheep.

The sketch-maps are unashamedly hand-drawn and are intended to be a simplification of reality and an aid to the directions. They are not always totally to scale but they serve their purpose, illustrating the main landmarks (and a few other interesting bits for good measure) to aid navigation.

Once you have done one or two routes, you will feel more confident and you may even be able to complete the whole book (no prizes, although I did lose a puncture kit somewhere near Hebden Bridge. If you find it you can have it). Good luck.

ABBREVIATIONS

L	left
R	right
J	junction
TJ	T-junction
XR	crossroads
N	north
S	south
W	west
E	east
PF	Pathfinder map – to indicate when a route continues on another map
BW	bridleway
FP	footpath

EXTENDING ROUTES

As this book is only intended as a guide to mountain biking in the W Yorks area, I assume that people will try out different routes and find ones which they like and then continue to use them. However, once you have found your favourite routes, it may be interesting to add on new sections to keep them fresh. One way of doing this is to purchase Pathfinder maps to the area and look for other bridleways that may be of use (see section on Maps).

The other way is to join up routes within the book. With a little imagination, it is possible to join up several routes to create one monster route. To help you, not only have I given suggestions below, but I have also indicated on the maps where routes join up. What a nice person I am.

JOIN: Route 2, 19 and 16
       End of 19 in reverse, 18 and last half of 17.
       19, 18 and last half of 17
       And any other combination you can think of.
       Route 10, 11 and 12

These are just suggestions of the more obvious ones that can be joined. Other combinations are possible depending on individual taste.

Key to sketch-maps

`\-_-~`	**Bridleway**
`~~`	**Road**
`\-_.-~`	**Footpath**
`∷∷∷`	**Made-up Track**
`-→→-`	**Steep Bit (in direction of arrows)**
`~~~↘`	**Stream**
`⤬`	**Bridge**
`◆`	**Building**
`\-_-~⊿`	**Link with other route**
`xttttt↗`	**Railway**
	Wood/Trees
	Water
	Urban Area
`△`	**Trig point**
`N` `⇑`	**North Pointer**

BRADFORD ROUTES

The 7 routes in this area all cover reasonably hilly terrain with the least height gained on Route 1, at 380 feet; this is still a reasonable climb, especially when compared with the routes over in Leeds, where the most height gained is 406 feet. The highest climb in the area is 1100 feet, one of the highest in the book and one of the longest in the book.

Not surprisingly, this means that most of the runs are fairly demanding and certain ones, such as Route 2, are also technically demanding.

Distances vary from 7.5 to 25 miles, although this does not necessarily reflect their difficulty.

Thus, the Bradford area offers a good variety of routes to suit all riders and particularly those who want a reasonably difficult run.

For sadists, there is always the possibility of linking up routes to create mega-routes which should satisfy even the hardest of riders. Details of these can be found in the section on extending routes.

Crossing the autumn moor   Photo: Steven Behr

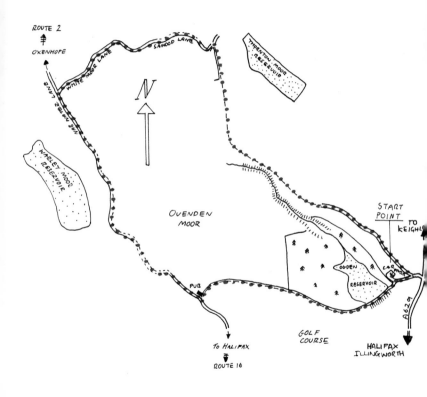

ROUTE 2
↑
OXENHOPE

SAWOOD LANE

WHITE MOOR LANE

THE NAB'ES LANE

THORNTON MOOR RESERVOIR

N
↑

WARLEY MOOR RESERVOIR

OVENDEN MOOR

START POINT
TO KEIGHLEY

CAR PARK

OGDEN RESERVOIR

PUB

↓
TO HALIFAX
↓
ROUTE 16

GOLF COURSE

A6204

↓
HALIFAX
ILLINGWORTH

1. OGDEN RESERVOIR

DISTANCE: 7.5 miles – off road 6 miles; on road 1.5 miles
TIME: 1 hour 20 mins.
GRADE: 2/2
HEIGHT GAINED: 380 feet
TERRAIN: Open moorland, rugged hill-farming area, quite
       exposed
SURFACE: Single-track, rough bumpy lanes and road
START POINT: G.R. 066 309 Ogden Reservoir carpark
O.S. MAP: Outdoor Leisure 21 South Pennines

This is a short but pleasant run containing quite a good variety of terrain. It starts off with a long stretch along gently sloping single-track, some of which can get a little tricky and it can get quite wet in winter. After a short downhill section, you move on to rough farm track. You then climb, using a road and finish off with a good fast downhill section on a bumpy track. It will suit most riders and could prove to be a good introduction to 'off roading' for novices, although it is important to remember that much of the route is in fairly exposed countryside. Much of this route is new, having only recently been given bridleway status. The area is quite popular especially with walkers so do take care particularly on the last downhill section.

Route Description
From the start point, head E back towards the A629, but before meeting the main road, turn sharp L, almost back on yourself to follow a walled lane that climbs gently to a small house. Follow this lane all the way along as it follows the walls on either side and passes through several small gullies. At the end of the walled section, continue on the track as it follows the steep-

sided stream bed on your L, until it veers off to the R as the stream valley becomes less severe.

Follow what is now rough single-track climbing at first. Then drop down to meet a wall corner where a blue waymarker can be seen on the wall and Thornton Moor Reservoir is visible to your R. Follow the track down with the wall on your L as it again runs between two walls and reaches a gate. Pass through the gate and follow the track down to the L with the wall on your L. The track bends R as it drops and then slightly L as it begins to level out. Stay on this track and follow it all the way to a road, Nab Water Lane.

At the road, turn L up the hill. Follow the road, passing Warley Moor Reservoir on your R as it climbs and then becomes fairly rough, cobbled and then back to tarmac again. After app. 2 miles you arrive at the Withens pub, where you take the BW which starts at the back of the carpark. (It is signposted as a FP but has recently been upgraded to BW, so the signs may not change for a while.) This wide track then descends all the way down to Ogden Reservoir where you cross the dam wall to return to your starting point.

Cobbles towards Withens Pub

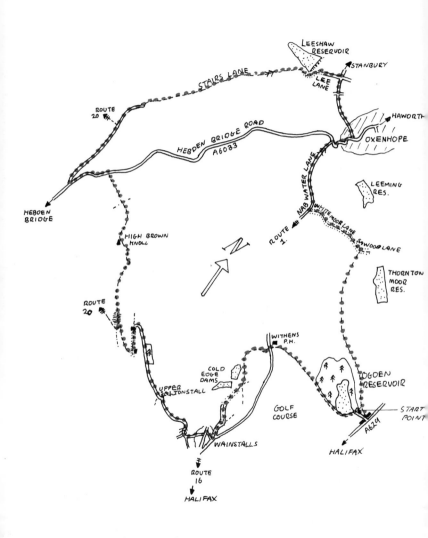

2. OGDEN RESERVOIR – STAIRS LANE

DISTANCE: 19 miles – off road 13 miles; on road 6 miles
TIME: 4 hours
GRADE: 4/4
HEIGHT GAINED: 700 feet
TERRAIN: Open moorland, quite rugged and hilly
SURFACE: Hardpack lanes, technical single-track and road
START POINT: 066 309 Ogden Reservoir carpark
O.S MAP: Outdoor Leisure 21 South Pennines

This is quite a difficult route and thus is only worth trying if you are proficient. It contains some nasty climbs and some very technical single-track, in a hostile and exposed environment. Having said that, for anybody who wishes to tackle it, it is a very enjoyable and scenic route which covers a wide variety of surfaces and riding; well worth a visit. This is one of my favourite rides but it can get quite boggy in winter and navigation can be difficult on the tops, so it is best left to a reasonable day and done with someone else. Excellent fun in the right conditions.

Route Description
From the start point, head E back toward the main road, A629. Before meeting the main road turn sharp L, almost back on yourself. Follow a walled lane that climbs gently to a small house. Continue on this lane as it follows the walls on either side and passes through several small gullies. At the end of the walled section, follow the track as it continues with the steep-sided stream bed on your L until it veers off to the R as the stream valley becomes less severe. Follow what is now rough single-track climbing at first. Then drop down to meet a wall

27

corner where a blue waymarker can be seen and Thornton Moor Reservoir is visible on your R. Follow the track down with the wall on your L as it again runs between two walls and reaches a gate.

Pass through the gate and follow the track down to the L with the wall on your L. The track bends R as it drops and then slightly L as it begins to level out. Stay on this track and follow it all the way to a road, Nab Water Lane. At the road, turn R and follow the road for 1 mile down to a TJ with the A6033 where you turn R. Keep to this road until you reach the village of Oxenhope. Here you need to take the first turn on your L following signposts to Stanbury and Colne. Then, as you climb up the other side of the valley, you go L at the XR along Lee Lane.

Stay on this road to Leeshaw Reservoir where it becomes more of a track. Then follow it up as it veers off L and starts to climb, gently at first and then more steeply as you pass a farm. Stay on this track as it levels out and then reaches the top of Stairs Lane. Go straight down until you reach a road. Head straight down and then follow along until you meet the A6033 at a TJ. You go L up the hill. Follow the road until you pass the Dog Kennels at the end of the walls and emerge onto the open moor.

Just after the first small, gravel lay-by, turn R to follow the vague, rough single-track up the hillside, just after the wall on your R reaches its end and heads up the hill. Although not obvious, the path is relatively easy to find, but quite difficult to ride especially on the top section where it is probably easier to carry. As the track gets to the top of the steepest section, it levels out a bit. Follow the track again, past the stone piles that help to mark it until you eventually reach the Trig Point (443m) at the top of the hill. From here, go to the standing stone a little further along the track. This point is the trickiest of the run in terms of navigation as there are no real distinct features by which to navigate. You are looking for a small single-track that goes to your R down the hill, forking off slightly. If you have a compass, the direction is SE. If not, the track can be seen as it heads down

The Withens Inn at the top of the climb from Wainstalls

the hill in the direction of the large valley in the distance.

Having chosen the right track, you should follow it down keeping to the L fork (most of the tracks up here are very narrow and difficult to see) until you meet the end of a drainage ditch. Follow the track L along the ditch to a small stone bridge. Here you turn R and follow the track down the hill as it follows a ditch/gulley much of the way. You eventually meet a small stream near a wall. Cross the stream (it may not be flowing in dry weather) and keep on the track following the wall/fence on your L. After passing through a steepish gulley, you arrive at a small path J where the wall that you have been following turns L and heads down the hill. Head down, following the L fork which bends L and then R as you descend, until you pass through a gate and then drop steeply to a single-track road near a house. Go L, pass through the gatehouse and swing R to follow the road out of the valley. Keep straight on until, after a mile or so, you climb a steep hill and then turn sharp L into the village of Wainstalls.

At the next J go L and then immediately R through the village. At the TJ turn L and quite soon L again following signs to the Moorcock Inn. Keep on as the road bends and keep L until you eventually pass through a gate onto a gravel track up to the dam. Keep on this track as you pass the dam. The track bends R by a derelict farm and then reaches another farm. After passing the second farm, the track climbs, bending first to the L and then R until you meet the road at the Withens Inn. Go straight across the road and take the BW which starts at the back of the carpark. (It is signposted as a FP but has recently been upgraded to BW so the signs may not change for a while.) This wide track then descends all the way down to the reservoir where you then cross the dam wall to return to your start point.

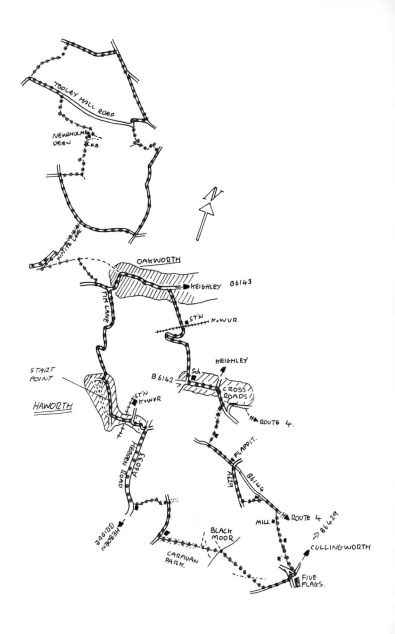

3. HAWORTH

DISTANCE: 20 miles – off road 10 miles, on road 10 miles
TIME: 3 hours
GRADE: 4/3
HEIGHT GAINED: 650 feet
TERRAIN: Mixture of open moor and hill farms, fairly hilly
SURFACE: Farm tracks, green lanes, single-track and road
START POINT: G.R. 032 372 carparks on hill, Haworth
O.S. MAP: Pathfinder 682 Bradford & 671 Keighley & Ilkley

This is a fairly varied route, covering quite a variety of terrain. Starting from the picturesque and tourist town of Haworth, famous for its Bronte connections and start of the Worth Valley Railway, you climb steeply out of the valley only to go down again to the village of Oakworth, with its period chocolate box Railway Station à la Railway Children (Send my love to Father). Then you have to climb again only to drop once more and then climb again to the final piece of open moorland before you drop once again to the village of Goose Eye. Again it is up and down and finally up a steep hill just to really finish you off before you go and sample the delights of Haworth. Although you only climb 650 feet, because you go up and down so many times, it seems a lot more. Hill-haters, this is not one for you. For others, it is a pleasant tour around what is a very beautiful area.

Route Description
From the start point, head down the hill to the station. As the road bends L, turn R and climb the steep road to a TJ with the Hebden Bridge road. Turn R and follow the road until it bends R. Here you turn L up the signposted BW to the L of the houses and follow this, climbing all the way until you reach a TJ

with another road. Turn R up the hill until shortly you reach a farm on your L. Turn L immediately past it and follow the BW past the caravan park until you reach a small gate at the start of some open moorland, Black Moor. Take the obvious track straight ahead. After passing through a gap in a wall take the R fork and follow this down until you meet a road at a gate. Here turn L to the TJ and then L by the Five Flags. Then turn R toward Bingley and then almost immediately L along the signposted BW to Haworth Road.

Follow this track downhill. As it bends L go straight on following the single-track past a couple of farms. Then climb uphill passing a mill and eventually to the Haworth road where you turn L. Turn almost immediately L again onto the BW at the next farm. Follow this to the end where you will meet another road, the Halifax road. Here you turn R and then L at the J by the Flappit toward Haworth, up the hill. Just after the brow of the hill, turn R down the BW signposted to Cross Roads. Follow this until you meet another road where you turn L down the hill and then L again toward Haworth. Then after a short while you pass Lees School on your R and you turn R down the hill toward Oakworth. Go down the hill and eventually up the other side until you meet a TJ where you turn L. Follow the road right through the village and leave the village as the road climbs and you pass Tim Lane on your L.

Shortly after this you see the walled BW to your R. Follow this as it bends almost immediately to the L and eventually meets a J with another track where you turn L up the hill. Follow the track until you meet a wood at a J. Here, turn sharp R, almost back on yourself and follow the track to the road. Turn L and follow the road until a road comes in from the L, and you turn R along the BW past the farm. Follow the track to where it bends to the R and the BW goes to your L downhill between a wall and a fence.

After passing through a small gate you drop steeply into the small, wooded valley and eventually over a bridge. Keep straight

35

The climb from Newsholme Dean

on keeping the wall and farm to your R. Then follow the track R up the hill behind the house until you meet another track near a gate. Turn L up the hill and follow the track a short distance until you reach a fork. Take the R fork which goes up the hill and runs up a sort of gulley. Follow the track heading uphill all the time until you eventually reach the road where you turn L. Then after a short distance the road bends to the L. Take the BW to your R up the hill until you pass through a small gate. You then cross a stretch of fairly rugged moorland until you reach another stretch of road and turn R. At the next J turn R down the hill until you reach a sharp R turn along Todley Hall Road.

After a L-hand bend the road climbs to a R-hand bend and you follow the track to the L along Clough Bank Lane. Head downhill until, shortly after passing a small house, you take the narrow track back to your L. Follow this down to a road in the village of Goose Eye.

Turn R and follow the road up the hill until you reach some XR where you turn R along Shack Lane. Eventually you turn L up White Lane which you follow along to a J near a wood. Here you turn sharp L along part of the route that you have already ridden and then turn R until you meet the main road. Then turn L and then R along Tim Lane. Keep on this road until after a climb you meet a XR at Haworth where you can go straight ahead through the village, or L down the hill to your start point.

BINGLEY-WILSDEN CIRCUIT

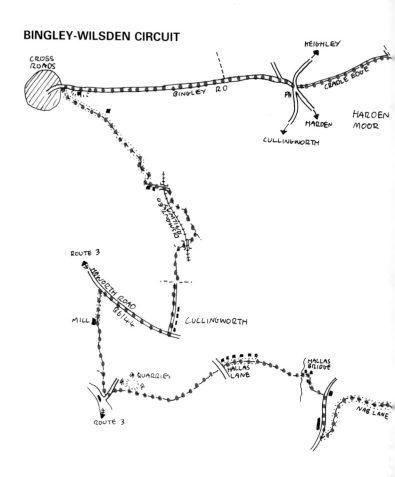

CROSS ROADS

KEIGHLEY

BINGLEY RD

PH

CRADLE EDGE

HARDEN MOOR

HARDEN

CULLINGWORTH

CULLINGWORTH

ROUTE 3

HAWORTH ROAD B6144

MILL

CULLINGWORTH

QUARRIES

HALLAS LANE

HALLAS BRIDGE

NAB LANE

ROUTE 3

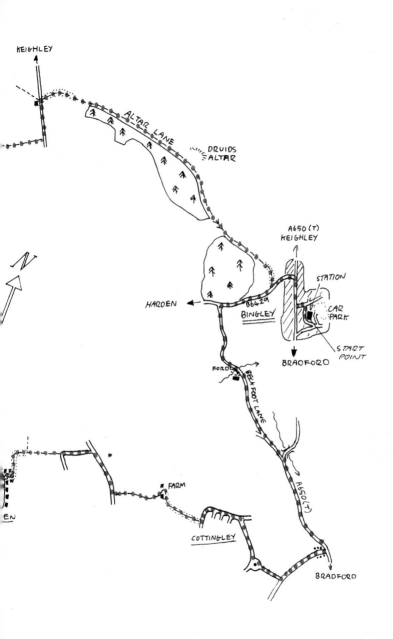

4. BINGLEY – WILSDEN CIRCUIT

DISTANCE: 14.5 miles – off road 9.1 miles, on road 6.65 miles
TIME: 1 hour 45 mins
GRADE: 4/3
HEIGHT GAINED: 672 feet
TERRAIN: Steep to rolling, open moorland and rugged
            agricultural
SURFACE: Mainly hardpack lanes, some single-track
START POINT: G.R. 109 391 Bingley Station
O.S. MAP: Pathfinder 682 Bradford

A good route which is challenging enough for the experienced as well as being possible for most newcomers. The route involves quite a lot of climbing although most of it is on fairly easy ground and the difficult climb is done at the beginning. Navigation is relatively easy as much of the route follows waymarked paths. There are several sections of fairly rough single-track which can be difficult to negotiate depending on the condition of the ground at the time; but much of it is on broad tracks and lanes. This is one of my favourite routes as it can be done quite easily from my house and makes a good training route. Worth a detour from any area and as with many of the routes in the area, it can be linked to others to make an even longer and more challenging route.

Route Description

From the station, go to the TJ and turn L to the lights. Then turn R down the main street. Turn L at the next lights, over the bridge and past the Brown Cow pub. As the road starts to climb, follow it a short distance until you reach a rough road going back sharply to your R. This is Altar Lane – follow this road all the way up the hill as the lane gets steeper and the surface changes from loose gravel to sand to deeply rutted mud. After

1¾ miles the track bends L and you meet Keighley road. At the TJ, turn L and follow the road down a short distance to a gap in the wall on your R signposted as a permissive BW. Follow the single-track which follows the wall down through some trees and then after a short climb, to a sandy path which forks to the R. Follow this to the top where you meet a J at a wall corner. Turn L following the wall on your R and fence on your L for ½ mile until you descend to a road again by the Guide Inn. Turn R to the J and then straight across following the road signposted to Haworth.

Follow this for just over a mile until, after quite a long downhill, you pass a garage built in an old quarry on your L, near Cross Roads. Immediately past this turn L up the lane signposted to Cliffe View. Follow this track until you cross a banked road and pass in front of some houses to a gate. Here you turn R and follow the wall. About halfway along, the track turns to the L at 90 degrees following a line of trees. Continue on single-track until again the path turns R down a little gulley to a gate by a pond. Go along the walled, gravelled track to the end of the pond. Keep L and pass open ground between 2 drives. Cross the bridge over the disused railway and turn R down the narrow track to a metalled driveway near a large house. Turn R downhill until you reach a lamp post near the bottom of the hill where a mud track goes to the R. Follow this in front of the pond and up under the bridge to a J with a larger lane where you turn L.

Eventually you meet a XR where you go straight on until you come to a road, the B6144. Turn R up the hill until you reach the signposted BW on your L. Take this and pass in front of the Mill Shop. Follow the single-track down and then up past a farm on to a lane and then to the B6429. Here, turn L down the hill and immediately R along the signposted BW which you follow all the way until you meet the B6144 in the outskirts of Cullingworth. Cross the road and go straight down Hallas Lane which passes in front of some houses and gets progressively narrower until it becomes quite bumpy and steep as it drops to a bridge. Cross the bridge and climb up the hill on the other side passing to the R of the houses. Continue up the hill until you reach Bents Lane and turn R up the hill.

As you reach some small cottages on your R you find Nab Lane back to your L. Take this and follow the contours of the hill. This track provides quite a sandy and easy ride until it drops down to Wilsden and reaches a TJ. Here you turn L down the hill to the next J where you turn L and almost immediately R down Smithy Lane. Continue round the lane until you meet the BW which you follow round. Keep straight up past the FPJ onto the short, rough climb and then to the gate on a road bend. Keep straight on down the hill and R into Lee Lane. After a short distance on Lee Lane turn L down the signposted BW, through March Cote farm and out on the fenced farm drive until you hit another road. Turn L, then R and follow the road round R to the large green roundabout by the shops. Go downhill to the main Cottingley – Bradford road.

Here turn L down the hill and then L again at the lights. Follow the road for ¼ mile and then take Beck Foot Lane to your L just before the road bends R to cross the bridge. Follow the lane across the ford or bridge and eventually to a TJ with a road where you turn R and head down the hill to retrace your route back to the start point.

Cullingworth   Photo: Bruce Rollinson

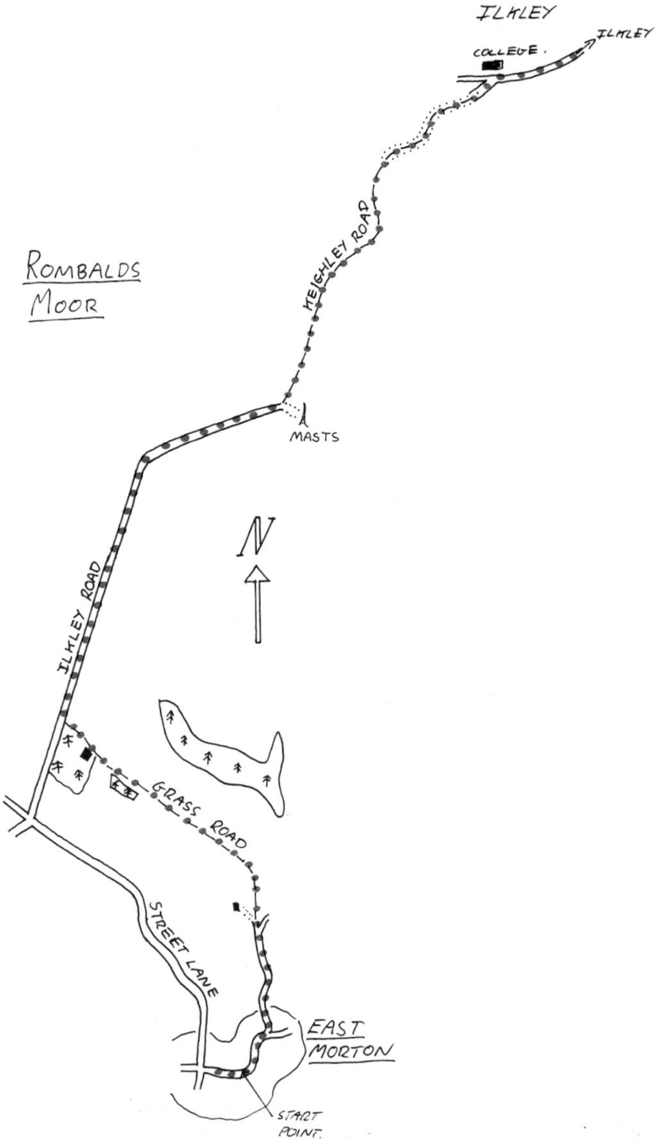

ILKLEY

ILKLEY

COLLEGE

KEIGHLEY ROAD

ROMBALDS
MOOR

MASTS

N

ILKLEY ROAD

GRASS ROAD

STREET LANE

EAST
MORTON

START
POINT.

5. ILKLEY MOOR

DISTANCE: 9.5 miles – off road 4.75 miles, on road 4.75 miles
TIME: 1 hour 45 mins
GRADE: 3/2
HEIGHT GAINED: 820 feet
TERRAIN: Moorland
SURFACE: Hardpack lanes with some single-track
START POINT: G.R. 099 421 East Morton
O.S. MAP: Pathfinder 671 Keighley & Ilkley

This route is not particularly brilliant in its own right. It covers around 9.5 miles of which half are on road and the rest are a mixture of loose gravelly track, farm track and Green Lane. It does climb quite a way, the worst section being the climb out of Ilkley which is a fairly long, steep slog.

The main reason for including it in the book, is that this is the only way across Ilkley Moor for mountain bikers. Although the moor looks like a good place to ride, there are no bridleways on it, thus it should, under no circumstances, be used. Furthermore, as a peat moor, the environment is a very delicate one. Mountain bike traffic would simply ruin what is a particularly sensitive and beautiful area. You simply have to look at the mess that has been made by walkers to realise that it should not be used.

Although the moor is not rideable, it still poses a large barrier for people in the Bradford area if they want to go up in to the Dales. Thus if you are looking for a route over Ilkley Moor, this is it. DO NOT GO ON THE MOOR.

Route Description
From the start point, follow the road N through the village until

you meet a road on your L on the brow of a hill. Follow this up a slight hill until you pass the last of the terraced cottages and you see a gravelled track to your L. Follow this up the hill. As the track bends L to a farmhouse, you continue straight up following the rough grassy lane that runs between the walls. The lane turns to the L and then runs more or less straight until it meets tractor tracks and eventually passes Upwood Hall Farm to meet Ilkley Road at a gate. Here, turn R and follow the road for around 1¼ miles until it ends close by some large masts. At this point, pass through the gate on the L and follow the unmade track heading NNW. This track drops all the way down to Ilkley. The last section of it is metalled. To return, simply retrace your steps.

Grass road and the road up to Ilkley Moor

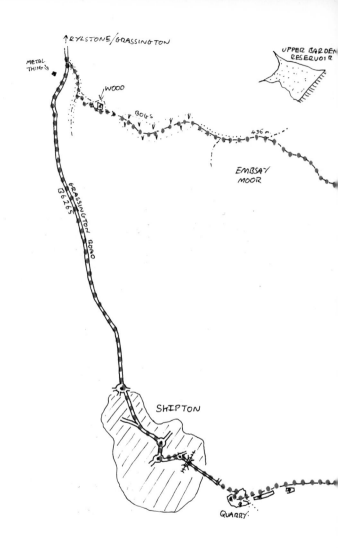

↑RYLSTONE/GRASSINGTON

METAL THING ↘

WOOD

BOGS

UPPER GARDEN RESERVOIR

436 m.

EMBSAY MOOR

GRASSINGTON ROAD

B6265

SHIPTON

QUARRY

ADDINGHAM – BOLTON ABBEY

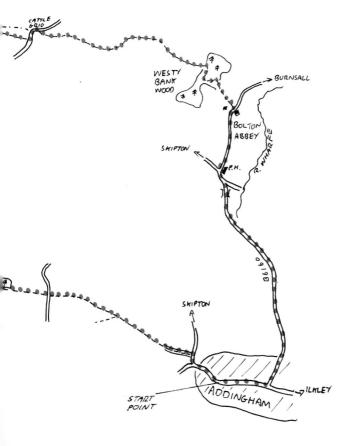

6. ADDINGHAM – BOLTON ABBEY

DISTANCE: 22 miles – off road 15 miles, on road 7 miles
TIME: 4.30 hours
GRADE: 5/5
HEIGHT GAINED: 1100 feet
TERRAIN: Open moorland, valleys and woods, rolling to hilly
SURFACE: Farm tracks, Landrover tracks and some single-track
START POINT: G.R. 075 498 Addingham Main Street. Pathfinder 662
O.S. MAP: Pathfinder 662 Bolton Abbey and Blubberhouses and 661 Skipton and Hellifield

This is probably my favourite route in the book. It is very varied, covering very different terrain and is quite a challenge in parts. There are two distinct sections to the run: Addingham to Skipton and Skipton to Bolton Abbey. The first follows what is almost a straight route climbing reasonably gently and then dropping the same way into Skipton. Most of this section is grassy lane which can be muddy in bad weather but is more than rideable. The second section really starts once you go off road after leaving the Grassington Road. Once on the top the scenery is breathtaking and it is almost worth the climb just for that (as well as the long downhill that follows).

The climb up is steep and difficult – not to say impossible in parts – as it crosses tussocky grass before it reaches the track. Then as it levels out, the track becomes single-track – crossing peat bogs for around a mile. This section of the route should definitely not be used in or after bad weather as the moor top is very fragile and it is impossible to ride due to the depth of the bogs which are also quite dangerous. Please do not use it except in good conditions. Thank you.

Addingham – Bolton Abbey

Route Description

From the start point, follow the main road W through Addingham village and then up the hill following the Skipton signs. As you leave the village, turn L along Moor Lane which you follow up until you see the R turn. Follow this on a narrow, metalled track and pass through 2 gates as you cross the main road. Follow this track as it climbs straight ahead and eventually passes through several gates and comes to a small road after 2 miles. Cross straight over the road and continue on the track heading W. The track follows an obvious route for another 2½ miles until it reaches Skipton. Towards the end of the track, you reach an old quarry and a small wood. Here the track turns sharply R and goes back down below the wood following a rough, walled track and then drops to a road. (PF 661) At the road, head straight down the hill, under the railway bridge to a mini-roundabout. Go straight on until you reach a roundabout at the end of the main street. Turn R to go up the main street and then, at the next roundabout, go L and follow the signposts to Grassington.

Leave Skipton and keep on the Grassington road for around 4 miles. As you start to see the crags up on your R, one of which has a cross on it, keep your eye out for a small metal tower in a field to your L. As you reach this, you see a signposted BW to High Bank on your R (the signpost is set back from the road). Follow this BW until you come to a signpost for an access area with a map next to it. Pass through the gate on your L and follow the signposts to Halton Height. The track is difficult to determine here but you need to head straight up passing to the R of the small wood. (The access road which passes to the L of the wood looks a much easier way up, but is NOT a public BW so DO NOT USE IT.)

Then join up with a track which carries you on up the steep climb through a gate and then as it levels out, on to the moor itself. The track is quite easy to follow but do watch out for the numerous bogs, especially the one with the warning sign which is only visible when travelling the other way. (THIS IS WHY THE ROUTE IS NOT SUITABLE IN WET WEATHER.) The route is marked with marker posts with blue arrows or blobs on all the way. It eventually reaches a Landrover track which you then follow heading in the same direction up the hill. Shortly after, the track becomes rutted and starts what is a very long and very enjoyable descent – it seems to go on for ever. Stay on this track all the way passing a couple of reservoirs on your L and still going down until you meet an unsignposted fork where you go R and then shortly come to the road.

Turn L down the hill and then R along the signposted BW to Bolton Abbey just after the cattle-grid. Follow the obvious path for 1⅓ miles. Then after passing through a gate cross the large field following the stones marked with the blue dots until you come to the wood. Pass through the gate and turn R to follow the signs down through the wood. Then cross diagonally L through the field to pass through the first gate. Follow the track through the next field round to the R and pass through the gate at the end near the buildings. Take the obvious farm track L down the hill to the road. Then turn R and head along the B6160, passing through the archway to the J near the pub. Turn L and then R and across the small bridge and follow the B6160 S until you arrive back in Addingham.

From the new road

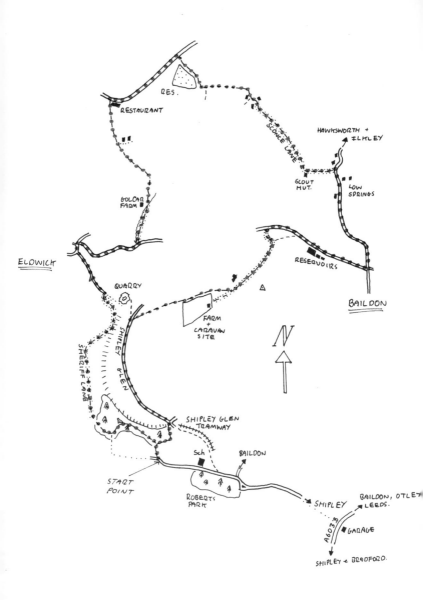

RES.

RESTAURANT

SCONCE LANE

HAWKSWORTH +
ILKLEY

SCOUT
HUT.

LOW
SPRINGS

GOLCAR
FARM

ELDWICK

RESERVOIRS

BAILDON

QUARRY

SHERIFF LANE

SHIPLEY GLEN

FARM
+
CARAVAN
SITE

SHIPLEY GLEN
TRAMWAY

Sch

BAILDON

START
POINT

ROBERTS
PARK

SHIPLEY

BAILDON, OTLEY
LEEDS.

A6038

GARAGE

SHIPLEY & BRADFORD.

N

7. BAILDON MOOR

DISTANCE: 9.5 miles – off road 8 miles, on road 1.5 miles
TIME: 1 hour 30 mins
GRADE: 3/2
HEIGHT GAINED: 850 feet
TERRAIN: Open moorland, low pastures, hilly
SURFACE: Hardpack lanes, rough single-track
START POINT: G.R. 133 386 end of Coach Road.
O.S. MAP: Pathfinder 682 Bradford (W. Yorks) and 671 Keighley
and Ilkley

This is my local route, of which I ride parts usually every week to keep fit. It is interesting, varied and challenging enough for the experienced; manageable for the not so experienced. The terrain is also varied with some quite hard climbs, fast downhills and everything in between. The route follows a mixture of hardpack track and rough single-track with a small amount of tarmac. Seasonal variations in weather, whilst not particularly affecting the hardpack, can change much of the single-track from dusty trails to mud. If this is the case, the road can be used from the wall end on the glen to the end of the farm access track to avoid churning up the ground. This route has the advantage of getting much of the climbing out of the way quite quickly leaving a nice gentle route with some good downhill sections. The route covers a rich historical area which spans the prehistoric to the present day. Along the glen, stone circles can be seen; along the wall of the caravan site, cup and ring stones; and on the moor, evidence of mining.

Route Description
From the start point, take the BW which starts near the point where the road becomes unmade (on your R as you come up the road and signposted rather interestingly as a FP). Follow the

sandy track to the top of the hill passing on your L a track where the route will finish. The path becomes quite rough at the top where there are the remains of old cobbles. At the top you reach open ground (Shipley Glen). Keep straight on and follow the line of the road keeping the wall on your R. At the wall end take the rough single-track which leaves the wall end on the other side of the road and climbs to the horizon where it meets another wall end at a caravan site. The track is often muddy and very hard going towards the top. (For those wanting a little diversion, instead of taking the track, keep straight on along the glen to a small quarry ideal for messing around and relieving pent up frustrations!)

From the caravan park, keep straight on, initially keeping the wall to your R. Follow the rough track to a rough road where you turn L and follow it down to a J with the main road (Bingley Road) and turn R downhill. After passing the reservoirs you arrive at a TJ where you turn L up the short hill and then down the other side. After 2 miles the road levels out and bends to the R. Here you turn L along Sconce Lane which is a rough, walled lane and cycle for ½ mile until the track forks in front of a cottage. Turn R, bear L and then R until another main road by Weecher Reservoir.

Turn L and after ½ mile L again immediately past the Croft Restaurant, signposted White Croft Farm. Follow the track straight down until it turns sharply L near 2 houses. Go through the small gate on the bend and follow the track through a field and 2 more gates until you reach the obvious BW at a third gate. Follow this, cross the beck by the farm and follow the track down to the road turning R down the hill. Turn L at the J and shortly L again down Saltaire Road. Follow the road down until a R turn up Lode Pit Lane to the J. Turn L down Sheriff Lane to the bottom where you keep straight on down the narrow cobbled path. Go straight ahead at a path J down a very rough path to a small reservoir which you pass in front of. Climb briefly to a well-worn track where you turn R to fork. Turn R to a BWJ where you turn R and retrace your steps to the start point.

LEEDS ROUTES

The routes in this area generally cover rolling farmland with the most height being gained on route 9 at 402 feet. This does not necessarily mean that the routes are easier than routes in other areas, as some of the terrain can be quite technical in places and some of the longer routes can be quite hard going especially in bad weather. This said, Leeds does offer good possibilities for the leisure cyclist or the novice as there are a good assortment of manageable rides for any ability. As with other routes, by putting several together, different and more challenging ones can be constructed.

Climbing up onto the moor   Photo: Steven Behr

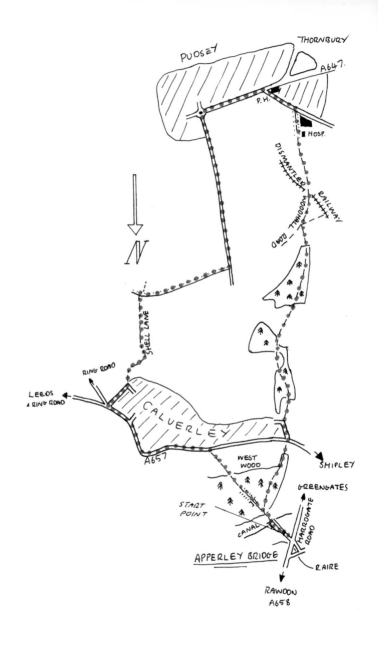

8. APPERLEY BRIDGE – THORNBURY

DISTANCE: 6.7 miles – off road 4.7 miles, on road 2 miles
TIME: 45 mins
GRADE: 2/2
HEIGHT GAINED: 394 feet
TERRAIN: Rolling farmland, woodland and urban
SURFACE: Mainly lanes with some single-track
START POINT: G.R. 195 379 Parkin Lane, Apperley Bridge.
O.S. MAP: Pathfinders 682 Bradford and 683 Leeds

This route is an interesting one and is one of my favourites. It is the shortest in the book and does not present too many physical or technical challenges, although it is difficult enough for newcomers to find it a nice challenge. The reason it is in the book is largely down to its location. The route lies right in between Leeds and Bradford and you are never really more than a few hundred yards away from a road. Having said this, the off road sections of the route are really surprising as you could be anywhere in the country as you cycle past farms and farm animals, where you might expect to see a typical urban landscape. It contains some reasonable climbs and a good long descent, if somewhat bumpy, and a good mix of lane and single-track. Although possibly not worth travelling a long way for, it is certainly worth a look if you are in the area; and a particularly nice 'Sunday afternooner' for a novice.

Route Description
Parking is possible along Parkin Lane, or in the surrounding area. Go along Parkin Lane and take the L fork of two roads that run next to each other. You then go over the bridge and straight on up a steep hill in to West Wood, under a bridge and to the

61

A657 where you turn L. Follow the main road until you reach a fork in the road with Calverley Lane and turn R up the slightly unmade Monson Avenue. At the top the road turns R and a narrow track goes off diagonally to your L. Follow this along a narrow, interesting, little section of single-track trying to re-member that you are actually in the middle of two large cities. At a small XR, turn R and follow this lane until you meet a main road. Turn L and continue S on this road until you come to the roundabout. Then turn R and follow the dual carriageway until you reach the second set of pedestrian lights. Cross the road and take Gain Lane next to The Junction Pub.

Turn R just before the large bakery and follow the road past The Dales Nursing Home. Go down the hill past the disused railway until you meet a J near a pub and a small house. Take the track that goes into the woods. Follow this Leeds Country Way through the woods keeping straight on until you meet a second gate in between 2 factories. Take the metalled road straight ahead and cross the main road once again. Go straight ahead taking the L fork through the gate. Keep straight on through the woods until you meet the road at a J near the bridge over the canal where the route started. Turn L to get back to the start point.

Shell Lane

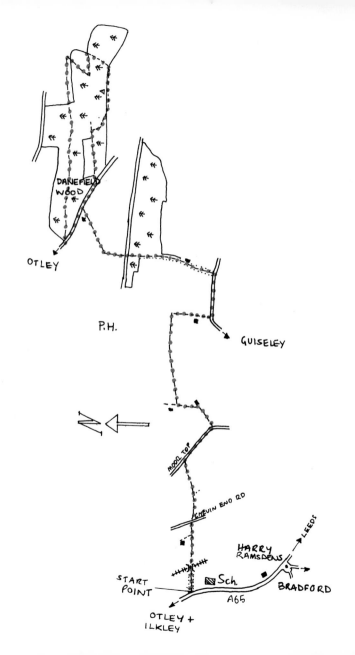

OTLEY

DANEFIELD
WOOD

P.H.

GUISELEY

N

MOOR TOP

CHEVIN END RD

LEEDS

HARRY
RAMSDENS

START
POINT

Sch.

BRADFORD

A65

OTLEY +
ILKLEY

9. MENSTON – OTLEY CHEVIN

DISTANCE: 9.5 miles – off road 8 miles, on road 1.5 miles
TIME: 1 hour 15 mins
GRADE: 2/2
HEIGHT GAINED: 402 feet
TERRAIN: Hilly farmland, quite cultivated, and woodland
SURFACE: Lanes, some hardpack, forest tracks and road
START POINT: G.R. 179 433 bridleway from A65, main road.
O.S. MAP: Pathfinders 671 Keighley & Ilkley and 672 Harewood

This is a pleasant, Sunday afternoon sort of run. It covers some
fairly hilly ground but is mainly on good surfaces and has the
benefit of some very good views. After the initial climb from the
start point, the run levels out to become fairly easy going,
especially around the forest. The Chevin Forest Park is a very
beautiful area and is popular with visitors all year round, thus
please be extra careful when riding around it. A definite
candidate for a picnic spot.

Route Description
From the start point on the main road, travel E down the hill
away from the road on the signposted BW. Cross the railway via
a bridge and carry straight on up the hill until you meet a road.
Go straight across the road carrying on up the hill on the
signposted BW. Again go straight on up the rougher track as the
main track bends to the R until you meet a TJ with a road, where
you turn R. Continue along the road until a R bend where the BW
is signposted off to your L. Follow the BW L in front of Moor
Farm and then R shortly after to follow the more level lane
which then bends R and drops to a road again. Turn L and
continue on this road for ⅓ mile until you reach another

signposted BW on your L. Follow this N to another road J which you cross going straight ahead. Then turn to the R on the marked BW which eventually drops to a road. Turn R up the hill to the carpark on your L.

You are now in the Chevin Forest Park which has a route specifically designated for horses. This is OK to ride and gives a good view of the forest. Take the R fork and head downhill until you come to a bend. Turn R and begin to climb. You eventually level out and then bear L to follow the outskirts of the forest. Keep straight on, keeping an eye open for the signs that say No Horses until you come to a TJ. Turn L down the hill and then take the second track on your L. Follow this and then turn sharp R until the track comes to the edge of a sort of cliff. Here you turn L and quite soon R down a short drop to a BW that brings you out eventually at the main road again. Turn L up the hill until you see the BW again on your R by Danefield House. You return to the start point by retracing the route.

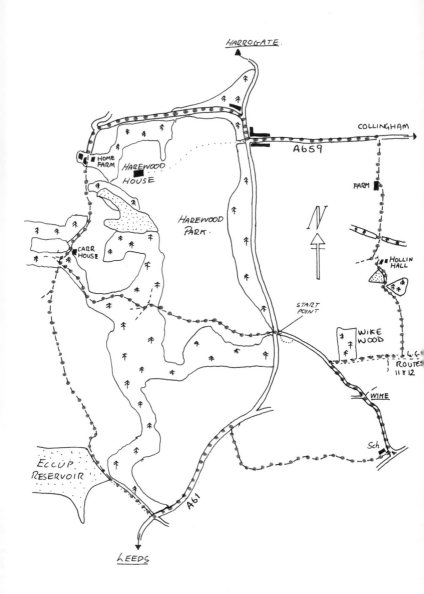

10. HAREWOOD

DISTANCE: 12 miles – off road 9.5 miles, on road 2.5 miles
TIME: 1 hour 30 mins
GRADE: 2/2
HEIGHT GAINED: 250 feet
TERRAIN: Rolling, mainly agricultural
SURFACE: Mainly wide sandy tracks with some single-track
START POINT: G.R. 325 432 crossroads on A61
O.S. MAP: Pathfinder 672 Harewood

This is another good 'Sunday Afternooner' with a choice of
endings. The terrain is generally rolling, thus it would suit
novices as well as leisure cyclists. What makes this route is the
scenery, particularly around Harewood House with its wooded
sections and open vistas.

Although quite a simple route, it should not be ignored by more
serious riders. There are some reasonable uphills and it passes
through some beautiful countryside.

Route Description
From the start point, follow the signposted Public BW W
through the large gate posts. Follow the obvious track straight
on towards the trees until you reach a gate at the entrance to a
wood. Shortly after you meet a TJ. Turn L following the
signposts along the sandy track to another J, where you turn R
along the clearly signposted Leeds Country Way. Following on
through the trees on the well-signposted path, you come to a

sort of XR where you take the R track (signposted Ebor Way). Go down the short hill to another J where again you turn R down the hill.

You will see a track to your L which you follow down single-track to a gate by a farm building marked on the map as Carr House. Here again follow the signposts across some open ground bordering Carr Wood until you meet a larger track. Follow this as it becomes metalled and you reach another J at the bottom of a hill. Here take the route straight up the hill that passes between 2 farm buildings. After crossing 2 cattle-grids you reach another signposted J where you turn R following the road for just under 1 mile to the main road. Turn R to the traffic lights at the entrance to Harewood House where you turn L toward Wetherby on the A659.

After approx 1m you see a signpost for a BW on your R, just after the lay-by and also signposted New Laithe Farm. As you approach the farm take the L fork and go through the farmyard keeping the buildings to your R. Follow the obvious track S downhill through several gates. After the fourth gate you cross a field towards the R side of Hollin Hall.

(There are changes underway to move this BW, as it passes through the garden of the farm. Once this happens, clear signposts will be erected to show the new route. **Then these instructions must be ignored**).

Pass around the R side of the buildings and then across the front of the dam of the small lake until you reach a gate at the far side by a wood. Go through the gate and follow the track up the hill. Keep the wood to your L until the track veers off R to meet a gate in the corner of the field.

Go through the gate and cross the field keeping close to the fence on your L. After meeting another track you come to a TJ where you turn R (signposted Leeds Country Way). Shortly after the track turns to the L. Keep straight on through the green gate and past the wood on your R until you meet the road once more.

Harewood House

Photo: Paul Hannon

Here you either turn R to find the start point – or go L, following the road through the village of Wike and then take the BW on your R just before the J. Follow it for 1 mile until you meet the main road. Here you turn L and then, as you meet a wood on both sides of the road, you turn R into the access road for Eccup Reservoir. Follow the track across the dam and then NW for 1½ miles to the woods at Stub House Plantation. Here you go R to follow the BW through Piper Wood and back to the start.

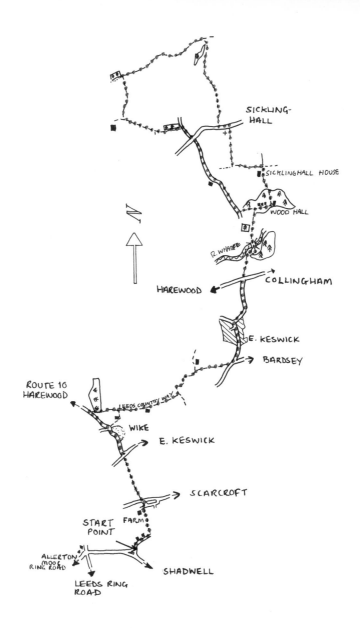

SICKLING-
HALL

SICKLINGHALL HOUSE

WOOD HALL

R. WHARFE

HAREWOOD ← COLLINGHAM →

E. KESWICK

→ BARDSEY

ROUTE 16
HAREWOOD

LEEDS COUNTRY WAY

WIKE

→ E. KESWICK

→ SCARCROFT

START
POINT FARM

ALLERTON
MOOR
RING ROAD

LEEDS RING
ROAD

SHADWELL

11. LEEDS – SICKLINGHALL

DISTANCE: 19 miles – off road 15 miles, on road 4 miles
TIME: 2 hours 30 mins
GRADE: 3/2
HEIGHT GAINED: 406 feet
TERRAIN: Predominantly rolling farmland
SURFACE: Hardpack lanes, some single-track and farm tracks
START POINT: G.R. 339 402 Holywell road
O.S. MAP: Pathfinder 672 Harewood

The longest distance route for this area. It is a reasonably challenging route which would possibly be a little too difficult for the novice. Covering rolling farmland, this route swaps and changes between hardpack tracks and quite rough single-track – and passes through some very picturesque countryside. It is a popular area with horses so take care as you go. Unfortunately, after prolonged periods of heavy rain, the horses hooves ruin some of the track making parts of it unrideable. It is unlikely that a mountain bike would cause so much damage, but it may be worth missing out after long wet periods.

Route Description
At the bend of Holywell road, take the signposted BW to the L and follow it as it bends R past a couple of farms until you reach a J near the gates to Barn Cottage Boarding Kennels. Take the less obvious walled and fairly rough single-track that goes down to your L and follows the line of trees until you reach a farm track. Here you turn R at the TJ by the farm. Then turn L on the bend of a road and follow it down until you meet a TJ. Go straight ahead down another BW which follows some single-track between trees until you hit some more tarmac. At what is

almost a staggered XR turn R and immediately L along Long Forge Lane. Follow the road through the small village of Wike and turn R to follow the **second** signposted BW to the R of Wike Wood. Keep straight on this lane which is later signposted as Leeds Country Way. Go through Low Green Farm and eventually through a couple of gates where you meet a TJ with another track. Here you turn L to head up along more single-track which soon heads downhill. After a few bends you meet a wider farm access lane where you go straight ahead until you meet the main road at a TJ.

Turn L down the hill to East Keswick. Cycle straight through the village, up the hill and take the R fork towards Collingham. Stay on this road until you meet a TJ where you turn R then immediately L down a BW which is signposted to Wood Hall and Sicklinghall. At the bottom of the hill take the R fork and cross the River Wharfe via the bridge. Follow the track up the other side to the TJ with another track – the start of the loop. Turn L and follow this track to the tarmac lane. Turn R up the hill to another staggered XR where you turn R then immediately L down the lane. After a short distance you turn L just before the gate posts, following the blue arrow to pass along the side of Addlethorpe Wood on your R. The track crosses a couple of fields and then returns to single-track again between hedges. Keep on this until you meet a better track leading to a farm. Here you take the gate on your R (at 90 degrees) and cross the edge of the field keeping the wall to your L.

After crossing several other fields you meet a J on the other side of a gate near the corner of a wood. Turn R here and follow the track alongside the line of the fence on your R. Continue following the track as it becomes slightly wider keeping straight on until you reach a small farm. Here you turn R following the BW signposted to Hollins Quarry. Keep straight on until you meet the main road at Sicklinghall. Here turn L and, just past the church turn R past Geecroft House. Take the R fork to find the BW which you follow until you turn L just after a sort of silage storage thing.

Sicklinghall

Photo: Paul Hannon

Follow the track until you meet the drive to Sicklinghall House where you turn R. Pass through the gates and turn L and immediately R, signposted East Keswick. Follow the track down and then up to a metalled track which is an access road to an hotel. Turn R up the hill and then follow the BW signposts. Pass through the small hamlet until after following the alternative BW signposts, you meet another track and turn L.

Go through a gate and return to the start of the loop. Turn L down the hill and cross the river to retrace your route.

SHADWELL – BARDSEY – SCARCROFT

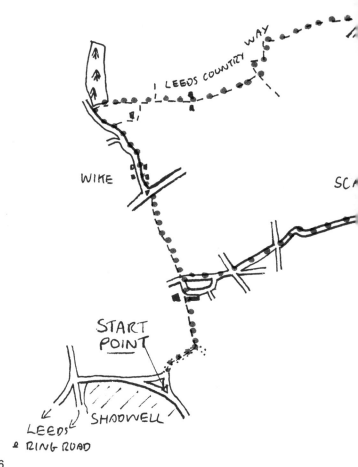

LEEDS COUNTRY WAY

WIKE

SC

START
POINT

LEEDS

SHADWELL

RING ROAD

COLLINGHAM
E. KESWICK

A58(T)

N

WOTHERSOME

THORNER

12. SHADWELL – BARDSEY – SCARCROFT

DISTANCE: 9 miles – off road 7 miles, on road 2 miles
TIME: 2 hours
GRADE: 2/3
HEIGHT GAINED: 352 feet
TERRAIN: Rolling farmland with some woodland
SURFACE: Well-used bridleway with some single-track
START-POINT: G.R. 339 402 Holywell road
O.S. MAP: Pathfinder 672 Harewood

This is a relatively easy route, which initially follows the course of route 11 as it rises and falls gently over a variety of surfaces. At Bardsey, as it changes direction, it follows for a short period the course of an old Roman Road and then turns back on itself. Quite a good introductory route or one that could be run in conjunction with others in the area.

Route Description
At the bend of Holywell road, take the signposted BW to the L and follow it as it bends R past a couple of farms until you reach a J near the gates to Barn Cottage Boarding Kennels. Take the less obvious walled and fairly rough single-track that goes down to your L and follows the line of trees until you reach a farm track. Here you turn R at the TJ by the farm. Then turn L on the bend of a road and follow it down until you meet a TJ. Go straight ahead down another BW which follows some single-track between trees until you hit some more tarmac. At what is almost a staggered XR turn R and immediately L along Long Forge Lane. Follow the road through the small village of Wike and turn R to follow the **second** signposted BW to the R of Wike Wood. Keep straight on this lane which is later signposted as

Shadwell – Bardsey – Scarcroft

Leeds Country Way. Go through Low Green Farm and eventually through a couple of gates where you meet a TJ with another track 1 mile from the last J. Here you turn L to head up along more single-track which soon heads downhill and after a few bends you meet a wider farm access lane where you go straight ahead until you meet the main road at a TJ.

Turn L down the hill and then soon R at the J and follow this road to a XR with the A58 in Bardsey. Turn R towards Leeds. After passing out of the village you climb a hill to some more houses and pass Rowley Wood. Turn L before a house and follow the BW to an old bridge. Here head straight down the hill through what was the bridge to a gate at the bottom of the hill. Pass through the R-hand of the 2 gates and cross the ford heading uphill on the obvious track through the woods between the fences until you meet a road. Cross the road and take the signposted BW on the other side. Keeping the hedge to your R follow the single-track along through two fields until you reach some woods. Follow the obvious track through the woods until you reach a TJ with a large track. Here you turn R and then very quickly L at the fork following the track through the trees. Follow this for ½ mile. Then as the track drops, you take a small track to your R which follows a small embankment and then takes you through a wood. As the track drops L to the Milner Beck, take the R fork by the big tree into a field. Turn L, following the signs and follow the hedge to the corner of the field. Then turn up sharp R again keeping the hedge to your L. At the top of the field, turn L and join the farm track which you then follow for 1 mile to the road.

Here, turn L and then R towards Scarcroft. Follow the road over the railway bridge and cross the main road carefully. Go straight across two XRs and then L up Brandon Crescent. As the road bends R again by the houses you go straight on and then L down the BW to retrace your route back to the start point.

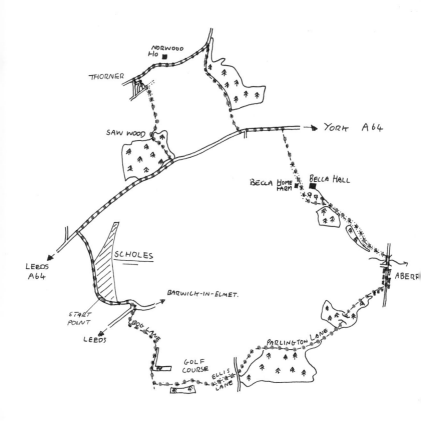

13. SCHOLES – ABERFORD

DISTANCE: 13.5 miles – off road 8 miles, on road 5.5 miles
TIME: 2 hours
GRADE: 3/2
HEIGHT GAINED: 226 feet
TERRAIN: Rolling farmland
SURFACE: Hardpack track and lanes
START POINT: G.R. 375 370, parking in Scholes
O.S. MAP: Pathfinders 683 Leeds, 684 Garforth and 672
          Harewood

As with most of the routes in this area, it is not really physically demanding as it covers rolling land. However, it is a nice ride for the leisure cyclist and a good chance to get some speed up for the more experienced. The route uses the A64 York road in 2 parts and riders must take extreme care as this is a very busy road; for this reason it would not really suit inexperienced riders. This aside, it is a very pleasant route.

Route Description
Park with care on the road in the village of Scholes. From the start point head N along the road out of the village towards the A64. At the TJ turn R and cycle for quite a way until you meet a lay-by on your L next to a wood. Here you turn L along the signposted BW at the end of the lay-by. Follow the track through Saw Wood until you meet a small gate at the other end. Pass through the gate and follow the obvious path N to a J with a larger track by some houses on the outskirts of Thorner. (This section is technically a FP. However, due to a problem which arose when the BW and the FP were swapped over, the BW shown on the maps and signposted L from the gate, is no longer

useable. Thus, the Leeds Countryside Service have agreed that this section can be used by cyclists until the problem is rectified. Please give way to walkers and keep your eye open for any new BW signs that appear.) (PF 672) At the J turn L and then R along the road. Then it is R, R, L and R to a TJ with a main road, where you go R. Keep on for 1 mile until the road bends L by a wood and you go R along a track with the wood on your L. (PF 684) Follow this until you meet a TJ with the A64 once again.

Turn L and then shortly after passing Woodlands Farm on your R take the BW on your R and follow it down. (Be careful crossing the road.) Follow the BW straight on down past Becca Home Farm until you meet a gate by a wood. Pass through the gate keeping straight on following the arrows until you meet a hardpack track at a J. Here you turn R along the signposted BW and follow it until you reach the village of Aberford. At the main road, turn R, cross the river and head up the main street a little way. You will see the BW to your R signposted to Throstle Nest Bridge. Follow this track keeping straight ahead past or through the tunnel and right on until you meet a road after 2 miles. Cross the road and take the BW straight ahead (PF 683). Follow it along past the chicken farm and eventually straight across the Golf Course. You reach single-track on the other side and follow the edge of a wood to a TJ with another track. Here turn R up the hill and stay on this track all the way until you meet the road near a J in Scholes. Turn R and then immediately L and follow this road to find your start point once more.

Married cyclists only?

BRIDAL WAY

THIS IS NOT A PUBLIC HIGHWAY

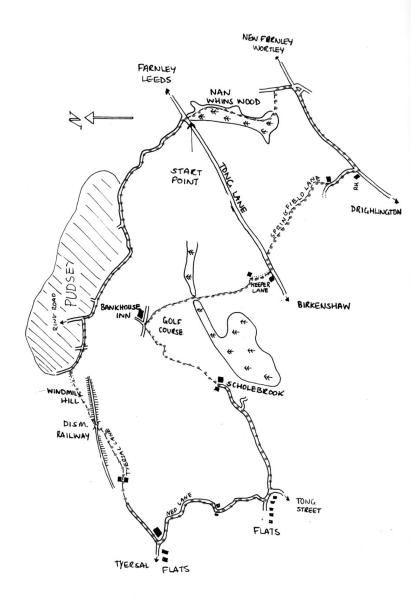

14. TONG – PUDSEY

DISTANCE: 10 miles – off road 5 miles, on road 5 miles
TIME: 1 hour 30 mins
GRADE: 2/3
HEIGHT GAINED: 300 feet
TERRAIN: Rolling urban and agricultural
SURFACE: Tracks, hardpack and some single-track
START POINT: G.R. 238 316 Lay-by on Tong Lane
O.S. MAP: Pathfinder 683 Leeds and 682 Bradford

This is a relatively easy route with about half the distance covered on road. The off road sections are mixed, ranging from single-track to broad, open tracks. There are some good downhill stretches although the route is fairly popular with walkers and horses so, as with all routes, make sure that you can stop. Uphills are not too bad and are all rideable although one or two may be a little too technical for the novice.

The great attraction of this route is its location. Although never really straying far from Leeds or Bradford, you really are in rural surroundings. Although there is a start point specified, the route could really be initiated from anywhere on its course. The route chosen has the advantage of a nice long downhill to finish it off and is best run in the direction suggested.

Route Description
There are several parking places on Tong Lane. From the start point, follow the signposted BW (it starts next to a FP – so do not get mixed up). Follow the BW up as it climbs several flights of steps and winds around through Nan Whins Wood until you eventually climb to a large gate system. Go straight on E up the hill to a TJ with a road. Turn R and then R again at the XR and

follow the A58 down the hill. Turn R immediately before the Valley Inn down Dale Lane. At the bottom take the R fork immediately past the farm buildings. Follow the BW as it bends up to the L following a hedged track and eventually meets a road. Here you turn L and then soon R up Keeper Lane (signposted as BW to Fulneck). At the top by the white house, take the L fork to head down the hill. At the bottom of the hill, cross the ford or metal bridge and head straight on up the hill on the narrow track following the signs for Fulneck. As you meet some houses, bear L up the hill passing a small row of cottages on your R.

At the top, you emerge on a road once more in front of The Bankhouse Inn. Turn L and then L again to follow the signposted BW back down the hill to yet another ford. Cross this and follow the broad lane up, through Scholebrook Farm and back onto the road at Scholebrook village. Follow the road up the hill for app. 1 mile until you reach the housing estate at a TJ. Turn R and then R again down the hill. Follow this road all the way up the hill on the other side of the valley. As you reach some blocks of flats, you turn R past a small factory and head along Tyersal Lane and down the hill. The surface of the lane deteriorates as it passes a couple of farms and then goes through what was an old railway bridge, through a gate and then to a ford at the bottom. Go through the ford and climb the gravelled track. After passing a row of cottages, you come to a TJ.

Here turn R and follow this road along until you reach another TJ. Again you turn R and follow the road as it starts to descend through the outskirts of Pudsey. After around 2 miles, you reach the TJ with Tong Lane where you started.

THIS ROUTE HAS NO IDEAL START POINT AND CAN BE RUN FROM ANYWHERE ON ITS COURSE.

Looking back on Tyersal Lane

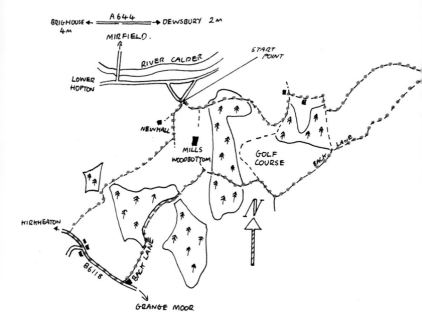

15. MIRFIELD

DISTANCE: 7.5 miles – off road 7 miles, on road .5 miles
TIME: 1 hour 30 mins
GRADE: 3/3
HEIGHT GAINED: 442 feet
TERRAIN: Hilly to rolling through agricultural and woodland
SURFACE: Hardpack lanes, rough track and some single-track
START POINT: G.R. 211 189 Bend in road
O.S. MAP: Pathfinder 703 Wakefield (south) and area

This is the only decent legal route that I could find in the Kirklees area. Several people very kindly suggested other routes but most of them turned out to follow FPs or other dubious routes. On speaking to someone from the Countryside Service for Kirklees, my fears were realised that there were no other routes of note in the area that were rideable. In fact Kirklees generally has a lamentably small amount of bridleway. With my humble apologies to the people of Kirklees, I respectfully submit this route for your enjoyment and just hope that more bridleways are upgraded soon.

This aside, the route is a very pleasant one, offering a variety of surfaces, scenery and riding styles. There are one or two reasonable climbs and some nice downhill. This would be a nice challenge to any novice.

Route Description
From the start point, follow the signposted BW SW up the hill towards New Hall Farm. As the lane bends R keep straight on through the gate and follow the single-track between the trees. Shortly after take the signposted track to the R through the gate

and follow the fence line through several fields and gates. Eventually you pass between 2 woods. Keep following the track as it bends climbing all the way until you eventually meet the B6118, where you turn L. Follow the road until, at the second farm you see a signposted BW to your L. Follow this through the farmyard and then down the hill on the walled track between two woods. As the track bends L you meet a gate. Pass through it and turn R, down the dip and then up the other side. Follow the track until after another gate you meet a metalled track on a bend. Continue down the hill to a TJ.

Here you turn R past the houses and then through the gate. Follow the track straight up through Whitley Wood. Shortly after leaving the wood you meet a TJ with another track and you turn R to a road. Here you turn L and follow the track for a while, keeping straight on as the road bends R. Follow the single-track through the trees alongside the Golf Course and start to drop as the path bends gradually L through a wood. Take the track that goes off to the R and follows single-track between a line of trees to a track J. Here turn L down to the farm which you pass on your R.

Follow the lane all the way down to the houses on the outskirts of Thornhill Lees. Just before you reach the houses you take the track to your L. Follow this past a farm and continue towards the field. Just before the field you will find a rough path between a line of trees heading for the wood. Follow this to the wood then turn R down the hill to a J. Turn L and follow this track past another farm and then L along the bottom of the wood. Then turn L up the hill as the road bears R to pass a farm and rejoin the wood once again. Shortly before reaching the end of the wood, take the track to your R and follow it down across part of the Golf Course. Cycle through a small wood, across another stretch of Golf Course and then into some more woods. Follow the obvious path which is marked with arrows through the wood and onto the road where you turn R to find the start point once again.

CALDERDALE ROUTES

As with Bradford, most of the routes in this area cover hilly terrain. This is hardly surprising with its Pennine situation. Most of the routes use fairly exposed ground, and make physically and technically demanding runs. Thus Calderdale has 2 routes which gain over a thousand feet, and even its lowest run is 440 feet. It also has the most technically demanding route – No. 20, and one of the longest – No. 19. All this helps to make Calderdale an extremely fertile and challenging area for Mountain Biking. See "Extending Routes" for more possibilities.

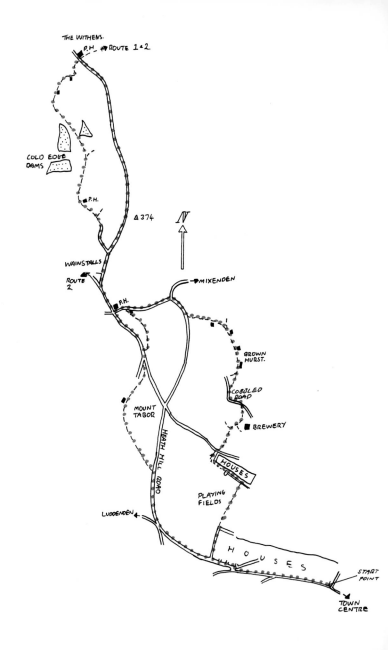

16. HALIFAX – COLD EDGE DAMS

DISTANCE: 14.2 miles – off road 5.7 miles, on road 8.5 miles
TIME: 2 hours
GRADE: 3/2
HEIGHT GAINED: 550 feet
TERRAIN: Urban areas, open moorland, hill farms
SURFACE: Road, farm tracks and rough single-track
START POINT: G.R. 073 253 Wellesley Park offices
O.S. MAP: Outdoor Leisure 21 South Pennines

Although this route has more on than off road, it still deserves a place in the book. Not the least because, like the urban routes around Leeds, it is always interesting to find off road around a town centre. Although not necessarily worth a detour, it should provide a bit of interest for locals. This route could also be joined with either the Ogden route or the Stars Lane route for that little extra something. The route is reasonably demanding with a long climb up to the Withens pub.

Route Description
From the start, head W straight up Gibbett Street which runs in to Roils Head Road. Then turn R and immediately L to continue up Roils Head Road until you turn R along Vicar Park Road. At the end of this road keep on going along a track with the wall to your R. At the TJ at the end, turn L. Go straight on past the bus turning circle and follow the path between the houses and the playing fields. At the end you turn R and follow the road to the bottom. Cross the main road and follow the obvious BW down on the other side.

Follow the track down and as it swings L into a wood, take the less obvious path straight ahead. Keep heading down with the

Halifax – Cold Edge Dams

Brewery to your R until you meet a road at a TJ. Turn L up the cobbled hill until just after the first house on the R. Here you turn R along the walled track. Follow the track taking the R fork to pass in front of Brown Hurst. Then go through the gate and straight on until you take the L fork up the hill, after you pass a farm on your R.

As you meet the road again, turn R along the road until you come to a J. Here you can turn R to Mixenden but you need to turn L and continue to the XR by the pub. At the XR turn R and follow this road up, keeping on the main road until you meet the Withens Hotel – at just over 1380 feet it is the highest pub in W. Yorks. At the pub, follow the track which descends from the opposite side of the road to the pub. It bends to the L and meets a gate. Then you bear R down the hill past Moorlands farm and follow the track more or less straight on past the next farmhouse and then as it bears L down past the Cold Edge Dams.

At the next gate, near a small settlement, keep straight on until the track you are following becomes road. Follow this to a J with the road you followed before to Withens Hotel, where you turn R down the hill. Then at the XR near the pub, turn L then R up the track immediately before the house. Follow this track to the TJ and turn R and then L at the road. Then as you reach the next J take the track between the R turn and the road straight on.

Follow the track past farm buildings until you once again reach Heath Hill road. Head R downhill and then L uphill at the next J. Follow the road down until you turn R and then L at the small J and head down to the start.

Cold Edge Dams from above

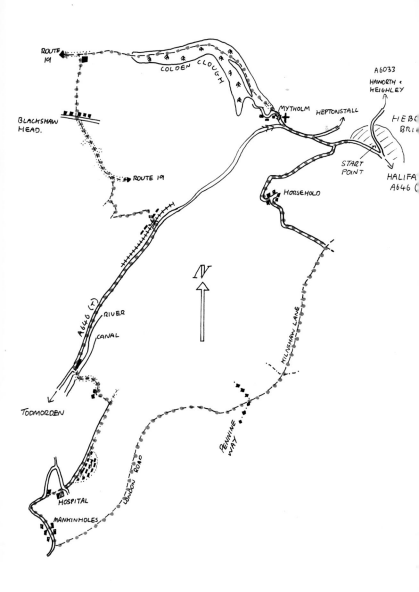

17. HEBDEN BRIDGE – MANKINHOLES

DISTANCE: 10 miles – off road 8 miles, on road 2 miles
TIME: 2 hours
GRADE: 4/3
HEIGHT GAINED: 770 feet
TERRAIN: Wooded valleys, hill farms and some exposed
         moorland
SURFACE: Hardpack tracks, some single-track, technical in
         places
START POINT: G.R. 994 272 Hebden Bridge carpark
O.S. MAP: Outdoor Leisure 21 South Pennines

This is quite a hard route physically, climbing 770 feet at least
twice during its duration; most of the climbing is done on good
surfaces but they do get quite steep. Despite the climbing, not
all the downhill is that fast as the first stretch descends on quite
technical surfaces. Due to the height gained, the views can be
spectacular and thus the route is very enjoyable.

Route Description
From the carpark at the start point, make your way to the A646
main road and head W up the valley towards Todmorden and
Lancashire, passing through the village. After passing the road
to Heptonstall on your R as you are nearing the outskirts of the
village, turn R up Church Lane. Head up the steep hill until the
road bends L and you carry straight on following the BW
signposted to Jack Bridge. Stay on the BW climbing all the time.
As the track forks, take the L fork up the hill again following
signposts to Jack Bridge. After, you reach a small, tarmac
section at Shaw Bottom where you turn L up the side of a farm.
Go straight on up, following the single-track between two walls.
As you meet Badger Lane at a TJ turn L then almost immediately R down the signposted BW, which follows a farm track
downhill. Stay on the main track keeping straight on past two L

turns. After a R bend the track meets a farm gate. Here you take the narrow track down L following rough single-track between the walls. The track then bends R and then does a hairpin L still going down. When you come to a sharp R turn you go straight ahead on the narrow track behind the small graveyard. Then go R and sharp L to keep on straight down the hill. Follow the track through the small group of houses and then as it bends to descend a narrow cobbled stretch (slippy when wet) to the valley bottom. Go under the bridge and on to the A646 where you turn R. Follow the road for app. 1 mile until you pass the road to Stoodley Glen. You soon reach a small terrace on your L and you turn down L immediately past this, looking out for signposts for a BW.

Cross the river and then the canal near the factory and then head up the hill taking the L fork (signposted as a private road). You then reach the Coach House and go L up the hill a short stretch to a TJ with another BW. Turn R towards Harvelin Park. Follow this BW along until it becomes a road and eventually reaches Stansfield View Hospital. As the road bends to the R, take the BW that carries straight on in front of the hospital and follows single-track to emerge on a road at a bend. Here you go straight ahead uphill and follow the road L to pass through the village of Mankinholes.

As the road leaves the village and bends R, take the BW to your L signposted Bridleway Hebden Bridge 3½. Follow this, climbing gently as the track changes from track to single-track to mud and back again a few times. Keep on up until you pass a farm on your L, shortly after a signpost for the Pennine Way – you then start dropping slightly. Carry straight on through a BWJ, past the houses and farm on your R. You eventually meet a J where a tarmac road descends to your L at a sort of XR of tracks. Take this road to the L and head downhill along the cobbles, through the small huddle of cottages and keep on down until you eventually meet the main road back at Hebden Bridge. Turn R and retrace your route.

The steep downhill from Blackshaw Head

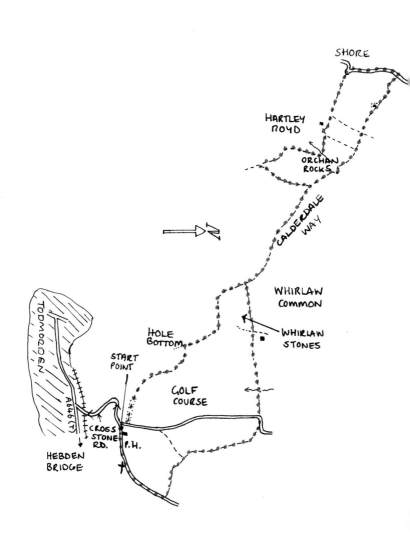

SHORE

HARTLEY ROYD

ORCHAN ROCKS

CALDERDALE WAY

WHIRLAW COMMON

WHIRLAW STONES

HOLE BOTTOM

START POINT

GOLF COURSE

TODMORDEN

A646 (T)

CROSS STONE RD.

P.H.

HEBDEN BRIDGE

N

18. TODMORDEN

DISTANCE: 7 miles – off road 5.8 miles, on road 1.2 miles
TIME: 1 hour 30 mins
GRADE: 3/2
HEIGHT GAINED: 443 feet
TERRAIN: Moorland and hill farms, open and rugged
SURFACE: Green lanes, single-track and hardpack
START POINT: G.R. 946 249 Pub, Cross Stone Road
O.S. MAP: Outdoor Leisure 21 South Pennines

This is quite a high level route commanding good views throughout. The route more or less follows the contours of the hills so that, although it does rise and fall, the climbs are not too severe – the initial one can be a bit laborious though. Just remember, the good thing about going up is coming down! The surface varies from single-track to quite wide and well-surfaced tracks with a section of old packhorse route for good measure – for those lucky people with suspension.

Route Description
From the start point, head E away from the pub and the small hamlet along the road past the cemetery. Follow the road along until you pass several farms on the R. You will see a track leading off to the L just past Rodwell Head farm. Follow this track up the hill skirting 3 farms, keeping them on your L. After about ⅔ of a mile, you reach a fork in the track where you turn L and meet the road. Follow the road downhill for a short distance. Then as it bends sharply L to go down the hill, you keep straight on the walled track that goes straight ahead. Stay on this obvious lane for ½ mile keeping straight ahead. Shortly after a J near a white farm building you pass through a gate

onto a piece of open moorland at Whirlaw Common.

Here take the path that leads off to your L at about 45 degrees and heads downhill. Follow it until you meet another track at a TJ near a gate. Turn R, go through the gate and follow the track as it goes along an old, roughly paved stretch and then becomes a walled green lane with single-track. This is Calderdale Way. Follow along it for ¾ mile passing the ruined farm building until you reach a sort of XR, where tracks join from the L and R. Turn L through the gate and follow the track down past Orchan Rocks. Go through a gate and, as the track bends sharply down to the L, take the less obvious track which goes off up the hill to the R and reaches a gate. Go through the gate and follow the track past the old quarry workings. As it splits take the L fork to cross an old stone bridge over Redmires Water and head towards an old farm.

As you reach the farm, you go through two gates and turn R up the track immediately after the second gate. Then follow this access track past several other farms until you eventually meet a road on a bend near Shore. Here turn R up the road and then turn R again after about ⅓ mile onto an access track. Follow this access track to a farm where you turn L just before the gate. Follow the single-track in front of the farm with the farm on your R. This track eventually becomes a lane again and you follow it right along to the gate where you emerged from Whirlaw Common on the way here.

At the gate, instead of retracing your tracks, head S down the hill following more of the old paving which gets very bumpy. Then go through a gate and straight on in front of the farm, through a small gate and then R down the hill when you meet the access track at a J. After going down this track for ¼ mile you meet another J where you take the track that climbs to the L of the track that you are now on, (it is signposted with a yellow arrow). Follow this track along the bottom of the Golf Course until you meet the metalled road which you follow. Turn R at the first J and L at the second to complete the route.

Causey, Whirlaw Common   Photo: Paul Hannon

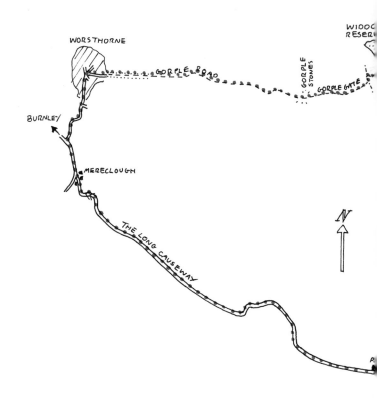

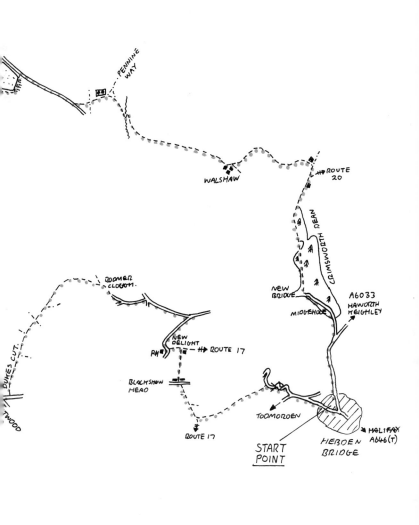

PENNINE WAY

WALSHAW

ROUTE 20

CRIMSWORTH DEAN

ROOMER CLOUGH

NEW BRIDGE

A6033 HAWORTH KEIGHLEY

MIDGEHOLE

DUKES CUT.

NEW DELIGHT

PH

ROUTE 17

BLACKSHAW HEAD

TWOOD

ROUTE 17

TOOMORDEN

START POINT

HEBDEN BRIDGE

HALIFAX A646(T)

19. HEBDEN BRIDGE – WORSTHORNE

DISTANCE: 24.5 miles – off road 15.5 miles, on road 9 miles
TIME: 5 hours
GRADE: 5/4
HEIGHT GAINED: 1105 feet
TERRAIN: Largely rough, exposed, open moorland
SURFACE: Single-track, grass, mud tracks, hardpack, road, you name it!
START POINT: G.R. 994 271 National Trust carpark Hebden Bridge
O.S. MAP: Outdoor Leisure 21 South Pennines

This is generally a fairly hard route in many ways. Not only is it reasonably long – 24 miles – but it covers difficult terrain and climbs around 1100 feet. The route starts off with a gentle climb out of Hebden Bridge and then levels out a bit before it climbs again quite steeply to reach the highest point. Although your hard work is rewarded by a nice long downhill, you then have to regain much of the height that you have just lost. The terrain at the highest point is also a bit on the boggy side so I would suggest that you leave it out during or soon after rainy periods. It must also be said that much of the ride is in quite exposed and lonely country and should not be attempted if the weather is looking at all bad. Having said all that, it really is a very interesting and picturesque run and one that you will probably find yourself repeating.

Route Description
From the start point, head N on the A6033, following signposts to Haworth and Keighley until you fork L and follow signposts to Midgehole and Hardcastle crags. Follow this road along until you reach a National Trust carpark on your R at New Bridge. You

then follow the track N as it bends R and shortly passes another carpark. Keep on this track, past the National Trust buildings on the R where the track becomes unmade. Go straight on N up the hill. After passing the end of the woods, you pass a farm on your R.

Pass through a gate by a ruined farm and turn L up the hill following the signpost. At the top of the hill, after passing through another gate, bear L following the signposts and follow the contours round the hill, Shackleton Knoll. Shortly after the track goes L through a gate and you turn R following the wall along a nice, long, grassy downhill to a farm at Walshaw. Keep straight ahead after the farm towards Clough Foot on the hardpack track at the other side. Keep straight on this track, take the bridge over Alcomden Water and then straight ahead up the hill on the concrete track. Follow the blue arrows and passing the wood on your R then descend to the road at some big gates. Turn R and head up the hill passing Clough Foot. When you reach the reservoir you turn L and cross the dam through the gates, then follow the track round the southern side of the reservoir.

The track then forks up to the L and meets another small J, where you turn sharp L up the muddy hill signposted Gorple Ruin and Worsthorne. Follow this track W for just over 3 miles to Worsthorne. The track starts off fairly technical then levels and broadens out and eventually drops on a good downhill section in to the village of Worsthorne. As you reach the village turn L and follow the road along until you meet a TJ. Here you turn L towards Hole Chapel – as you come to the small village of Mereclough, turn L up the hill by the Kettledrum Inn towards Blackshaw Head and Heptonstall. This road is the Long Causeway. Keep on this road as it climbs steeply at first and then more gently. After 5 miles you will pass Eastwood Road on your R and shortly after, you turn L up the signposted BW. Follow this along past several R turns until you meet a fork where you take the track to the L through the gate. Follow the deeply rutted track down, bearing R along a muddy track and past the farmhouse on your R.

Then after a sharp L bend on a made-up track, you reach a small row of cottages (Rodmer Clough) on your L.

Continue on this tarmac section to a bridge where you turn L up the hill and then R at the TJ at the top. At the next J, turn R down the hill. Then as you pass the New Delight Inn at the bend take the signposted BW to your L a short way up the hill. Shortly after turn R immediately before the house. Then follow the rough BW S up the hill and down to a road. Turn L and then R down the BW then take the second turn on the L. Follow this road all the way along past a small group of houses and down to the road. Here, go R down the steep hill, past the church and then L at the bottom back into Hebden Bridge.

Rodmer Clough   Photo: Paul Hannon

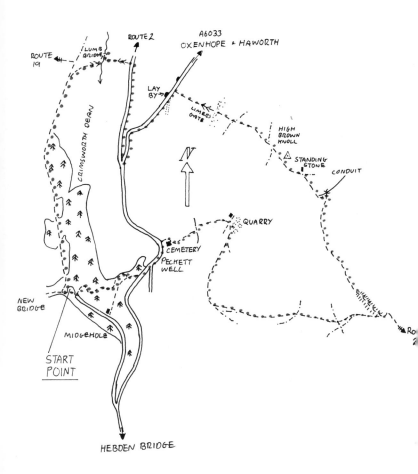

20. MIDGEHOLE – PECKETT WELL

DISTANCE: 8 miles – off road 6.7 miles, on road 1.3 miles
TIME: 2 hours
GRADE: 4/5
HEIGHT GAINED: 1000 feet
TERRAIN: Hilly, exposed moorland, difficult to navigate
SURFACE: Some hardpack, mostly rough, difficult, single-track
START POINT: G.R. 989 292 National Trust carpark, New Bridge
O.S. MAP: Outdoor Leisure 21 South Pennines

This is one of my favourite routes because it is technically quite demanding. Although fairly short at only 8 miles, the route usually takes a couple of hours or more. This is partly due to the difficulty of navigation in parts of the route, and partly because there are some nasty climbs to negotiate. Much of the route is single-track and not straight at that, thus speeds are low, not helped by the terrain which is often quite boggy. This route is definitely one for more experienced riders – novices will find it a little too difficult to enjoy. It is also one that should be approached with caution in bad weather and should be left out altogether if the ground is very wet for environmental reasons.

Route Description
From the lower carpark, head N up the hill following the tarmac track as it bends R and shortly passes another carpark. Keep on up this track, past the National Trust buildings on the R where the track becomes unmade. Continue straight on up the hill keeping the same direction all the way. After passing the end of the woods, you go past a farm building on your R – then before reaching the next farm, you turn R by a BW signpost and head almost diagonally down the hillside (signposted Lumb Bridge).

Midgehole – Peckett Well

Follow a rough walled track, past a ruined farm and eventually down to the bridge in the valley bottom near the waterfall. Cross the bridge and follow the track round on to the opposite side of the stream. Then at the wall end, turn L up the hill following the very roughly cobbled, steep path that is extremely difficult to ride.

At the top, you meet the road at a TJ where you turn R up the hill. At the next J, turn L up the hill on the A6033. Follow the road until you pass the Dog Kennels at the end of the walls and you emerge on to the open moor. Just after the first car pull-in turn R to follow the rough single-track up the hillside – just after the wall on your R reaches its end and heads up the hill. Athough not obvious, the path is relatively easy to find, but quite difficult to ride especially on the top section where it is easier to carry. As the track gets to the top of the steepest section, it levels out a bit. Follow the track again, past the stone piles that help to mark the Trig Point (443m) at the top of the hill.

50 yards before reaching the Trig Point, bear R and drop down 50 yards to skirt it, following the contours of the hill. You will then pick up a narrow track heading downhill from the standing stone. This point is the trickiest of the route in terms of navigation as there are no real distinct features by which to navigate. You are looking for a small single-track that goes to your R down the hill. If you have a compass, the direction is SE; if not, the track can be seen as it heads down the hill heading in the direction of the large valley in the distance. Having chosen the right track, you should shortly see (after several hundred metres) a BW marker post which you should be heading towards. (If you do not see one in 500m, retrace your route and try again.) Pass the post and then as you reach the end of a drainage ditch, follow the track L along the ditch to a small stone bridge. Here you turn R and follow the track down the hill as it follows a sunken lane for much of the way.

You eventually meet a small stream near a wall. Cross the stream (it may not be flowing in dry weather) and keep on the track following the wall/fence on your L. After passing through a

The steep bit down from Peckett Well

steepish gulley, you arrive at a small path J where the wall that you have been following turns L and heads down the hill. Here you turn R and almost double back up the hill. Follow this track and at the next small J take the lesser R fork and continue up the hill keeping the shooting butts away on your L. The track is very narrow and quite twisty but again there are marker posts to follow. As the track starts to drop, you pass a farm on your L and then you eventually meet a wall near another farm. Follow the wall along past several farms until you eventually reach a new, steel gate near an old quarry spoil heap.

Pass through the gate, keep R and pass through another gate to a J with a farm track. Head L down the hill until you reach a sort of staggered XR where you turn L and immediately R. At the next J at the corner of a small cemetery, turn L and drop down to the road. Here go L down the hill and past the pub. Shortly after passing a road on your L, turn R down the steeply cobbled, signposted BW which can be very slippy in wet weather. After descending for ⅓ mile, you see a track off to the R. Follow this, crossing the bridge and follow it up and then down until you reach the road at the bottom. Here turn R and return to the start point.

Looking back to Lumb Bridge and Crimsworth Dean

OTHER INFORMATION

Clubs and shops
Clubs or groups aimed at mountain bikers are generally very different in their composition and aims: from organisations aiming to represent its members on issues such as access and rights of way; to groups purely interested in the promotion of the sport. The one problem with these clubs and groups is that they do not allow for the many different needs of the individual mountain biker. Below are a couple of organisations which may be of interest to riders in this area. Keep your eye out as new ones appear all the time, and some pack up – as did the Yorkshire Mountain Bike Club during the writing of this book.

The British Mountain Bike Federation BMBF
The BMBF is the National Governing Body of Mountain Biking. Founded in 1990, this non-profitable organisation, (based at the Headquarters of the British Cycling Federation in Kettering) aims to develop the sport and cater for the needs of mountain bikers. In return for a membership fee, the BMBF represents mountain bikers at all levels with regard to access and rights, provides legal advice, third party insurance, including racing and many other benefits. The BMBF also organises races on a national basis and membership also includes a racing licence – a must for any prospective racers. Further details can be obtained from:

British Mountain Bike Federation
36 Rockingham Road
Kettering
Northants
NN16 8HG

The Aire Valley Mountain Bike Club
Based in Keighley and operated from Aire Valley Cycles, this club operates on a local level to encourage and promote mountain biking in the Aire Valley area. Club membership is £5 per year and entitles you to take part in all their events at a reduced fee as well as a 10% discount in the shop. Events are well-run and informal, and usually take the form of races up on

Penistone Hill near Haworth, on the second Sunday of every month from March to September. Winter activities are also organised and include Maintenance classes and trips to events. The club is well worth joining as it still retains the fun element which mountain biking is really all about. Further details from:

Aire Valley Cycles
102-104 East Parade
Keighley
0535 610839

There are many cycle shops in West Yorkshire, all offering different levels of service and products and different people have their favourites. I have tried to include only those shops which have a genuine interest in mountain bikes and which are local to the routes used – that way if you need anything when you are out, you know where to go. My apologies to any I have left out, it's nothing personal.

Ellis Briggs
18, Otley Road
Shipley
0274 583221

Chevin Cycles
Gay Lane
Otley
0274 462773

Cycle Gear
New Road
Halifax
0422 344602

61/63 Wharfe St
Sowerby Bridge
0422 831676

Cycle Sport 2000
3/5 Water St
Skipton
0756 794386

Keith Lambert
108 Main St
Bingley
0274 560605

Stif
The Loft
Granby St
Headingley
Leeds
0532 789606

Wharfedale Cycles
37 Leeds Rd
Ilkley
0943 607957

Maverick MTB
229 Bradford Rd
Leeds
0532 394595

AIRE VALLEY

C Y C L E S
SPORT & LEISURE

Main Agents for:

MARIN – KONA – ORANGE – PACE – RIDGEBACK – ALPINE STARS –
G.T. – DIAMOND BACK – SCOTT – MBK – SHOGUN – M.T. SHASTA –
OFF ROAD – CLASSIC – SARACEN – PEUGEOT DIA-COMPE –
EMMELLE – OAKLEY – X-LITE – D'ARCS – SALSA – MANITU –
ROCKSHOX – ANSWER – SHOCKTECH – HOPE TECHNOLOGY –
MERLIN – NUKE PROOF – CRUD CATCHER – CRUD CLAW –
SUNTOUR – CAMELBACK – ROHLOFF – SEDIS – HEADCASE – ONZA –
MAGURA – PORKYS MAVIC – ARAYA – RIDGIDA – STICKER PACKS
SHIMANO SERVICE CENTRE.

MOUNTAIN BIKES BMX **TOURERS RACERS** **Lay By & Christmas Club**	*VISA/ACCESS* *SWITCH*

SALES–SERVICE–REPAIRS–SPARES
Accessories & Clothing   :   Wheel Building

102–104 East Parade, Keighley, BD21 5HZ
Tel. (0535) 610839 – Fax: (0535) 690119

THE NORTH'S FINEST CYCLE COMPLEX

OTHER ERNEST PRESS MOUNTAIN BIKE GUIDES

DERBYSHIRE AND THE PEAK DISTRICT
by TIM BANTON, ANDY SPENCER, & TOM WINDSOR

Contains 21 **easily accessible and legal** routes, varying from 7 to 40 miles and providing rides for the family as well as for the young, fit biker. The authors have taken great care to establish the legality of each route and give detailed explanations of rights of way, bridleways and other terms. Each route is circular, has clear instructions and is illustrated by a two-colour sketch map. Photographic illustrations also show the varied character of the terrain, from gritstone moor through limestone dale to wooded parkland.

ISBN 0 948153 12 1   Illustrated soft cover   £6.50

THE LAKE DISTRICT, THE HOWGILLS AND THE YORKSHIRE DALES
by JEREMY ASHCROFT

Presents 36 selected routes amongst England's finest mountains; some completely new, some established classics. All levels of ability catered for...routes across summits, passes, moorland and along valleys. Rights of way explained along with the OFF-ROAD CODE, conservation, clothing, equipment, maps, and accident procedure. Each route is well illustrated with freshly drawn maps in 2 colours, b&w photos. Clearly written route descriptions.

ISBN 0 948153 10 5   Illustrated soft cover   £7.50

MORE ROUTES IN THE LAKES, HOWGILLS & DALES
by JEREMY ASHCROFT

This author's first book is widely recognised amongst the mountain biking fraternity as a model guide and received rapturous reviews from the biking magazines. His second volume brings 36 more new routes, all carefully checked for legality and catering for all levels of ability. Two-colour maps drawn specially and to high standards, with photographic illustrations for all routes.

ISBN 0 948153 13 X   Illustrated soft cover   £7.50

NORTHUMBERLAND
by DEREK PURDY

32 well researched, totally legal routes throughout Northumberland, the best kept mountain biking secret in England.
Bridleways, forest tracks, old drove-roads, ancient commercial routes, and neglected county roads.
Each route beautifully illustrated with black and white photos, two-colour maps, accompanied by technical terrain analysis and plotting plan, clearly written route descriptions including a little local history and colour.
There are routes for all abilities, with options to link some together to extend the challenge if you are feeling fit!

ISBN 0 948153 16 4   Illustrated soft cover   Price £7.50

To order by mail please send a cheque made payable to The Ernest Press with 10% added for post and packing.

The Ernest Press, 1 Thomas St., Holyhead, Gwynedd LL65 1RR.